THE
AZTEC MYTHS

THE
AZTEC MYTHS
A GUIDE TO THE ANCIENT
STORIES AND LEGENDS

CAMILLA TOWNSEND

Dedicated to my students, past and present.
I thank you for the joy you have brought me.

HALF-TITLE Jade rabbit from the Dumbarton Oaks collection, Washington, D.C. The Aztecs loved the rabbit and allowed him various metaphorical meanings, some of them humorous. This one has a phallic eagle warrior emerging from between his legs.

FRONTISPIECE Man-sized eagle warrior from the Instituto Nacional de Antropología e Historia in Mexico City. Originally brightly colored, this impressive terracotta piece was found at the site of the Templo Mayor.

First published in the United Kingdom in 2024 by Thames & Hudson Ltd, 181A High Holborn, London WC1V 7QX

First published in the United States of America in 2024 by Thames & Hudson Inc., 500 Fifth Avenue, New York, New York 10110

The Aztec Myths: A Guide to the Ancient Stories and Legends
© 2024 Thames & Hudson Ltd, London

Text © 2024 Camilla Townsend

British Library Cataloguing-in-Publication Data
A catalogue record for this book is available from the British Library

Library of Congress Control Number 2023944879

ISBN 978-0-500-02553-6

Printed and bound in China by Toppan Leefung Printing Ltd

MIX
Paper from responsible sources
FSC® C104723

Be the first to know about our new releases,
exclusive content and author events by visiting
thamesandhudson.com
thamesandhudsonusa.com
thamesandhudson.com.au

CONTENTS

Cuauhtitlan

▲Teotihuacan

●Texcoco

Azcapotzalco
●

Tlacopan ●

Tlatelolco
●Tenochtitlan

Coyoacan ●

▲Cuicuilco

●Chalco

Iztaccihuatl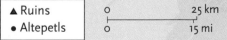

Popocatepetl

Cuernavaca
●

| ▲ Ruins | o ——— 25 km |
| ● Altepetls | o ——— 15 mi |

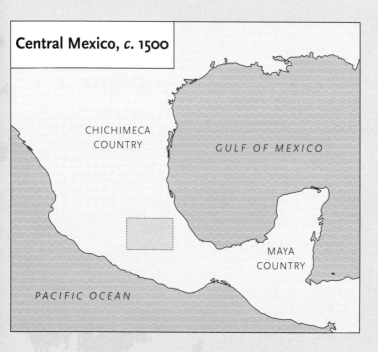

Central Mexico, c. 1500

CHICHIMECA COUNTRY

GULF OF MEXICO

MAYA COUNTRY

PACIFIC OCEAN

Tlaxcala •

Malinche

Cholula •

Huexotzinco •

• Cuauhtinchan

Tecamachalco •

1

WHAT ARE THE AZTEC MYTHS?

> 10 House. In this year Huactli died, he who had been ruler
> of Cuauhtitlan. He had been ruler for sixty-two years! He
> was a ruler who did not know how to plant corn for food.
> Nor did his subjects know how to make textiles. They still
> wore hides. Their food was just birds, snakes, rabbit, and
> deer. They did not yet have houses. They just kept going
> from place to place, kept moving on…[1]

Few cultures are generally understood to have been so controlled by their religion as the Aztecs of Mexico, and few religions are envisioned as being as violent and as celebratory of death as theirs. In textbooks as well as popular lore, the story goes that the Aztecs believed that the universe would collapse if they did not feed the gods by practicing brutal human sacrifice. Because of this, continues the usual narrative, the Aztecs were universally hated by their neighbors, who therefore were delighted to side with the Spaniards when the Europeans appeared on the scene in the early sixteenth century.

Readers may be surprised to learn that although there is a kernel of truth buried in this narrative, it is distorted almost beyond recognition. The story is largely what the invading Spaniards wished to believe themselves—and wished the world to believe—about the people they had conquered and were continuing to treat harshly. Aztec religion, the surviving evidence indicates, was actually comprised of a variety of rich and compelling traditions. Human sacrifice did have a place within the whole, but not in the way that it is generally portrayed. This book will offer a guide to the Aztecs' myths based not on assertions that have been made—and continue to be made—by outsiders, but rather, on the stories the Aztecs wrote down in their own language for their own posterity not long after the arrival of the Europeans.

A BRIEF HISTORY OF EARLY CENTRAL MEXICO

During the last Ice Age, with its attendant lower sea levels, there existed a land bridge between today's Siberia and today's Alaska. Between about 15,000 and 11,000 years ago, in at least three successive waves, distinct populations of Asians crossed the Bering Strait, ultimately peopling the Americas. As the ice melted and the ecological environment changed, nomadic hunter-gatherers moved ever further south, seeking not only game but also nutritious plants that now grew abundantly and could be gathered easily. As these migrating groups became isolated from each other, they developed distinct language families and unique cultures.

In about 1500 BCE the Olmecs, located on the northern coast of Mexico's isthmus, seem to have become the first people in the hemisphere to dedicate themselves to a sedentary lifestyle based on full-time farming, relying on a combination of corn and beans to yield a complete protein. As is always the case when people settle down permanently, a division of labor arose and a wide variety of technologies (including writing, irrigation, and architecture) soon followed. It is important to note that this same shift had occurred at least five thousand years earlier across the Atlantic in the Fertile Crescent, where the presence of a constellation of especially protein-rich plants (notably, wheat and legumes) had encouraged people to become farmers sooner than anywhere else. The farming lifestyle had then spread to both Europe and Asia. Much later, when the people of Eurasia and those of the Americas came face to face, this head start in the varied technologies that accompany sedentary life would render it possible for the European explorers to subjugate the people of the Americas in a political and economic sense. But that remained millennia in the future.

The Olmecs are famous for their large carvings of the heads of great chiefs or gods.

The artisans of Teotihuacan crafted striking face masks.
This one is of shell mosaic.

In the meantime, the Olmecs with their agricultural society developed an impressive cultural repertoire. Their calendar, glyphic writing system, and craftwork awed their neighbors. Olmec influence spread eastward to what would become Maya country, as well as westward to a remarkable circular basin enclosed by a ring of mountains (often called the Valley of Mexico). There, a series of different city-states devoted to farming rose to dominance and then were successively brought low.

The grandest of all the cultures in the central basin was the city of Teotihuacan (Tay-oh-tee-WA-kan) whose magnificent ruins can still be visited. Scholars know relatively little of Teotihuácan, in the sense that there are no surviving texts for us to read. But the archaeological remains reveal a great deal about the residents' cosmology as well as their economic lives. Teotihuacan was the center of a long-distance trade network that extended northward to what is today the United States and southward to Central America. When their government

The archaeological remains of the city of Teotihuacan
are now a UNESCO World Heritage Site.

collapsed in about the year 650 CE, word of the fall spread far and
wide. The power vacuum instigated invasions by nomadic peoples
from the northern deserts, who were sometimes escaping warfare,
sometimes seeking more fertile lands.

Those deserts lay in what is now northern Mexico and southwestern United States. Speakers of languages in the Uto-Aztecan
linguistic family, especially the language called Nahuatl, comprised

the majority of the successive streams of people who made their way south to the central valley. These migrations took many generations to accomplish. It is probable that no single person traveled from today's Arizona to today's Mexico City. As the migrating groups made their way south, they often settled for a while in a particular region, intermarrying with the local populace, adopting some of their ways, listening to their stories. Then they would move on again if disagreements or outright warfare rendered it necessary.

13

Above: Carvings of the feathered serpent adorn Teotihuacan's surviving pyramids. *Below*: Living quarters and ceremonial spaces were full of vessels like this tripod ceramic piece.

The Mexica (Me-SHEE-ka) were among the later Nahuatl-speaking ethnic groups to arrive in the fertile central basin. (Indeed, in their own accounts, they were the very last.) They got there at some point in the thirteenth century. By then, the area was quite crowded, and for many years, the Mexica remained an itinerant people, willing to hire themselves out to others as a fighting force in exchange for the right to hunt some deer and plant a little corn. In the early to mid-fourteenth century, they managed to establish a permanent town on an island in the great lake that filled the center of the basin, and soon after that, they celebrated the formation of a kingly line.

Still, the Mexica remained relatively weak and vulnerable. The central basin's dominant city-state at the time was Azcapotzalco (Az-ka-po-TZAL-ko), populated by Tepanec people (who also spoke Nahuatl). In the early fifteenth century, Azcapotzalco's long-time king died. In the ensuing commotion, an underdog faction of the Mexica cleverly allied with a faction of Tepanec people who seemed otherwise to be about to lose all power. Together, working with allies from a third city-state called Texcoco (Tesh-KO-ko), they engineered a great reshuffling of power in the valley. From that day forward, the Mexica were the most powerful players in the area, and they continued to work closely with their Tepanec allies (who lived in a settlement called Tlacopan) as well as their allies from Texcoco. Historians have dubbed their relationship the Triple Alliance; it was the beginning of what we know today as "the Aztec empire."

For the next century, the Mexica and their allies dominated the central basin and gradually expanded their control to include almost all of today's central Mexico and much of the rest of Mexico. They established trading outposts in the far northwest of Mexico and as far south as the coast of today's El Salvador, leaving place names in

A sculpture from an incense burner found at Teotihuacan.
Probably the god of fire.

This early post-conquest drawing of the twin pyramids of the Aztecs' great temple relies on pre-conquest iconography.

Nahuatl throughout that still exist today. Tenochtitlan (Te-noch-TEE-tlan), the island capital, grew to be a wealthy and beautiful city, known for its gleaming pyramid temples visible from afar, its huge market, its orderly streets laid out in a grid, its rooftop gardens, and even a zoological collection maintained by the king. Storytellers and musicians entertained people around fires late into the evenings.

Beginning in the late 1490s or early 1500s, the Mexica heard rumors of strangers exploring the islands off the Yucatan peninsula. In 1517 and 1518, Spanish exploratory expeditions made landfall on the coast of central Mexico. And in 1519, a man called Hernando Cortés landed near today's Veracruz. Cortés gradually made his

Pronunciation Guide

Three rules will help English speakers pronounce most classical Nahuatl words relatively easily. First, the "tl" consonant is pronounced very softly at the end of a word: In English, the nearest equivalent is a simple "t" sound. Second, when "h" is followed by the letter "u," the intent is to produce a "w" sound. (Both of these rules are illustrated in the word Nahuatl, pronounced "NA-wat.") And finally, the letter "x" represents our "sh" sound. Since this is a common consonant in Nahuatl, this is worth remembering. For instance, the people we often call Aztecs called themselves the Mexica, pronounced "Me-SHEE-ka," and the word "xochitl," meaning flower, is pronounced "SHO-cheet." The stress is almost always on the penultimate syllable.

In the first section of the book, parenthetical guides to the pronunciation of Nahuatl words are provided. But after that, to avoid the proliferation of distracting parentheses when they may no longer be needed, readers are left on their own to sound out the names in the beautiful language of Nahuatl.

The Aztecs loved flowers. This drawing was made by an Indigenous artist working for the Franciscan friars after the conquest.

way toward Tenochtitlan, using what the Indigenous perceived as an extraordinary armed force to attract as many allies as he could. Moctezuma, the high king of the Mexica, sent out emissaries, but was unable to persuade Cortés not to come to the capital. So it was that the expeditionary force entered the city of Tenochtitlan in November of 1519. The Europeans lived as honored guests for over eight months, but violence between the visitors and the Mexica warriors broke out eventually. More Europeans continued to arrive, and the sight of them convinced increasing numbers of Indigenous towns to join them. After a protracted war, the newcomers demolished much of Tenochtitlan. Yet within months, Mexico City began to rise on the old city's foundations, built by Indigenous laborers and artisans, and the city folk returned to their homes, their memories of the old days still quite intact.

WHO EXACTLY WERE THE AZTECS?

The word "Aztec" has been bandied about since the eighteenth and nineteenth centuries, when scholars first began to treat the people of central Mexico as a subject of study. But no people ever actually called themselves "Aztecs." The scholars seized on a word they found in a tiny handful of documents: it was a term that referred to the people who had supposedly lived in the Mexicas' mythical ancestral homeland far to the north, called "Aztlan" (see Chapter 3). But they repurposed the term and used it to talk about the Mexica themselves, as if it had been their name. Soon others picked up on the usage, and it developed a life of its own. Today, almost everyone refers to the people whom the Spaniards met in central Mexico as the "Aztecs."

Why did the early scholars use this inappropriate term? And why did their readers like it so much, and pass it on? These are not questions we can answer with absolute certainty, but the term did have certain obvious advantages. By then, the word "Mexica" had long since led to the use of the term "Mexico" to refer first to the colonists' capital city and thereafter, by extension, to all of New Spain, as the Spaniards called their colony. After independence, the same term was incorporated by the country formally named the United States of Mexico. So there would have been a certain confusion in writing about the ancients as the "Mexica." Moreover, having a somewhat vague, fungible term like "Aztec" allowed scholars to allude not only to the Mexica, but also to the unit they formed with their close allies, or even to all the people they governed—depending on what a particular scholar was trying to communicate.

Unfortunately, the term's very flexibility has bred substantial confusion. It is sometimes impossible to tell who exactly a writer is referring to. The Mexica alone? The members of the Triple Alliance and other close associates? All the people in the central basin, and their nearest neighbors over the mountains whom they knew well? Perhaps even all the people over whom the Mexicas' state apparatus exercised some degree of control? Some people even treat the word "Aztecs" as interchangeable with "Nahuas," meaning speakers of Nahuatl, but that is problematic, as many Nahuatl-speaking migrants to places throughout the country we now call Mexico had nothing to do with the Mexica.

In this book, the word "Aztec" refers to all those Nahuatl-speaking people who lived in or near Mexico's central basin and interacted with each other regularly in the two centuries before contact with Europeans. The Mexica eventually became the dominant people, but they shared their lives with numerous other groups, with whom they traded, intermarried, and fought. All along, the myriad ethnic groups told each other their stories, and together, those stories form a corpus of Nahuatl-language narratives from that era. Each ethnic group had its own distinct tales, with varying degrees of overlap with others, but they were all part and parcel of the same cultural universe.

HOW HAVE SCHOLARS STUDIED THE AZTECS?

The vast majority of the scholars who have studied the Aztecs in the past have not been able to read Nahuatl themselves and instead have consulted archaeological remains, colonial-era painted or glyphic sources, and texts written by the Spaniards. Many of the books they produced have been exceedingly valuable in their time. The sources upon which they generally relied, however, were unreliable in important regards. The Spaniards were only too eager to depict the Indigenous people—and not just the Mexica—as having been barbarous in the extreme, and thus of having been in veritable need of conquest. Some of the statements they made are downright laughable. Bernal Díaz, a foot soldier who accompanied Cortés and wrote an account when he was an old man, once said, for instance, "Their pet snakes were fed on the bodies of sacrificed Indians and the flesh of the dogs that they bred. We know for certain, too, that when they drove us out of Mexico [City] … they fed those beastly snakes on the bodies [of our soldiers] for many days."[2] As preposterous as this example is, scholars have not laughed at everything reported in similar circumstances; many doubtful assertions have made their way into serious work.

Itzcuintli

The Aztecs bred little dogs (*itzcuintli*, or sometimes *xoloitzcuintli*) mostly to serve as food in times of need, but in some cases, when the people became close to them, they became pets. It has sometimes been said in modern times that the family would kill a pet dog when its master died, so that it could help him cross the river to the land of the dead. But that is not actually what an Aztec who still remembered the old days said. He recalled that when they had to kill a dog for food, the owner was sad. "The owner of the dog who had died placed a [symbolic] cotton necklace on him, stroked and caressed him, and said, 'Wait for me! You will ferry me across where there are nine layers [of the universe? of the underworld?].'"[3] This pragmatic man knew that his family needed the meat; he was also extremely devout. At the same time, he loved his dog.

Mexico's Xoloitzcuintli breed of dog remains popular today.

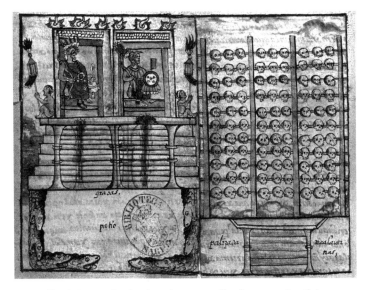

Bloody images showing Aztec human sacrifice figure prominently in
post-conquest texts. This drawing of a *tzompantli* (skull rack) appears
in a book by the Dominican friar Diego Durán.

Archaeological remains and colonial-era glyphic paintings, on
the other hand, are indisputably the creations of Indigenous people
and need to be taken more seriously. The difficulty is that they are
very lopsided in what they represent. Most archaeologists do not
dig up the sites of humdrum daily activity, such as markets where
copper sewing needles and obsidian jewelry were sold. Instead,
they have focused on the largest pyramid temples, which were the
scene of at least some human sacrifice (see Chapters 2 and 5). But
without being able to hear what the people were saying, we do not
know the context: How often did this happen, and at whose hands?
What did most people think of the practice? Were there any who

opposed it? What were some other important elements of their religious tradition? Likewise, the painted colonial-era codices, as the illustrated books recovered from this period are called, can be illuminating. But again, without being able to hear anyone speaking in full sentences, what we can deduce from them is quite limited. Many are even the works of late-colonial Indigenous people trying to paint histories and practices that they perceived to be "traditional," though many generations had passed since the people in the area had had anything to do with such practices.

In recent decades, many scholars have become increasingly dedicated to studying what are called the "alphabetic" sources written in the Nahuatl language. First, we must clarify: given that the pre-contact Aztecs produced only glyphic writings, how is it that we have such things? The answer is quite simple. Almost immediately after the initial military victory over the Mexica, Franciscan friars embarked on the task of teaching young Indigenous students the Roman alphabet. They wished them to learn to read so that it would be easier to teach them about Christianity. The students did as they were asked and became extremely adept in the new form of writing. Many continued to work for the friars for years, and others aided the parish priests or went to work for the Spanish court system. Today there are scholars who study the extraordinary Nahuatl-language religious texts produced by the friars and their Indigenous aides working together, and others who devote themselves to analyzing the mundane Nahuatl texts produced by the Indigenous making use of Spanish law in their wills, land sales, tax records, and so on. All of this work helps us to understand how Indigenous people in the colonial era thought and functioned in the multiple arenas of their hybrid world—how they were influenced by the Europeans, and how they in turn influenced the newcomers.

What has been missing, more often than not, is a study of sources produced absolutely without reference to the Spaniards—that is, those records produced entirely "off the radar" of the Europeans. What, in short, did the Nahuas talk about when they were among themselves, and were not responding to the needs or questions of the Spanish world? The best examples of this phenomenon are the histories written down by Nahuas for their own posterity. They had an old performative tradition—the *xiuhpohualli* (SHOO-po-WAH-lee)— in which a series of speakers would use painted glyphic timelines as mnemonic devices to elicit complex oral accounts. In this genre, composed mostly of recitations of history, a performer might pause and sing a relevant song, or lapse into the present tense and recite a dialogue, almost like a play. When a speaker covered a period of crisis—a war or a major disagreement, and especially if there were still differences of opinion about the matter—he would stop, and the same period would be covered again by another speaker from another lineage or town, or even by two or four other speakers if a variety of groups were to be knit together by the performance. In the mid-sixteenth century, the students who had learned the Roman alphabet used it to transcribe performances of these histories. They went home, consulted the elders, and wrote down their words. These written texts became the basis for a long tradition of keeping written "annals," histories that generally began with these old segments but often continued into the writers' own lifetimes. Spaniards usually did not even know their Indigenous acquaintances were keeping such histories, and they certainly were not a serious influence in their production. Of course, these sources are in some ways the

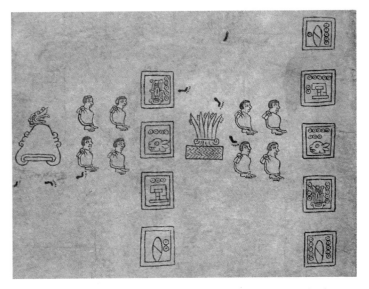

The Codex Boturini is a very early post-conquest Indigenous text closely based on a pre-conquest *xiuhpohualli*.

product of a Christian era, in the sense that the Christians had already arrived when they were written down, but they were by no means Christian in character, at least not most of the time. If we approach them thoughtfully, they will reveal to us a great deal about the pre-conquest world.

These texts mostly help us write history, but they can help us with an additional project as well. Written in Nahuatl for a Nahua audience, they often began in the deep or mythic past and touched on spiritual elements of life before proceeding onward to political events. They can therefore serve as an important source of information on Aztec religion. Yet scholars of religion have not made extensive use of them. Instead, just as one might imagine, those who have studied

Aztec religion have tended to proceed much as have other Aztec scholars—that is, they have focused on the archaeological sites and the texts written in Spanish, either by Spaniards or by *mestizo* (mixed-heritage) people of later generations. One of the most consulted texts has been the *Histoire du Mexique*, an anonymous French-language description of what its author claimed were Mexica religious beliefs. It was almost certainly taken from a Spanish-language account that was in turn based on a text produced with at least some Indigenous participation, as much within it is consistent with other native texts. But many of its elements are unique and even discordant with what Indigenous people said elsewhere, which renders the text more than a little suspicious. Nevertheless, it has remained a favorite.

Listening to what the Spaniards had to say, scholars for many years believed that the Nahuas had a tradition of believing in a "soul" that was very much like that of the Christian imagination. They cited the Nahuatl word *teyolia*, meaning something like "animating principle." Recently, however, scholars have carefully combed through this word's earliest usages in the sixteenth century, and have found that it was almost certainly a term elicited by Spaniards and then elaborated upon by them as they sought to project commonalities that might be useful to them in their conversion efforts.[4]

The result of proceeding in our studies by relying largely on Spaniards is that we have long accepted a picture of Aztec religion that is on one hand confusing and contradictory (due to the mixture of disparate sources, both hostile and sympathetic) and on the other hand deeply alien (due to the primary reliance on the pyramid-temple sites and the assertions of the Spanish conquerors). What might we learn if we paid careful attention instead to the religious stories the Aztecs told when they were among themselves?

PUTTING NAHUATL-LANGUAGE STORIES AT THE CENTER

In an ideal world, this book would be based on the screenfold pictographic books that were once stored in palaces and temples in the Aztec world; but we do not live in an ideal world. About sixteen pre-contact Mesoamerican books survived the bonfires of the crusading Spaniards. Of those, none is from the central valley (though one set of three texts, called the Borgia group, seems to have been rooted nearby). Sadly, however, even if we were to discover a cache of surviving books, we would not be hugely better off, in the sense that scholars still use a lot of guesswork in trying to read the pre-contact graphic representations. Such sources, which were mnemonic devices designed to elicit a volley of words, simply do not allow us to hear anyone speak in full sentences. Based on the images, we can hear the priests intoning calendrical dates or the names of gods, but that is all—no verbs, no narratives.

The Codex Fejérváry-Mayer is one of a handful of pre-conquest books
from the central Mexican culture area (usually called "the Borgia group")
to have survived the bonfires of the Spaniards.

In an effort to bring us one step closer to the religious stories the Aztecs told, this book is based only on sources written in Nahuatl that contain segments of old recitations as transcribed in the early colonial era, or else that offer self-conscious reflections about what seemed to have been lost or to be changing in the new era. (Most of the sources used fall into the former group, but a few into the latter, especially toward the end of the book.) Almost all of these texts are examples of the *xiuhpohualli* tradition described above—sometimes called the "annals" genre—or, at the very least, they contain elements that show the profound influence of that genre. None was produced in response to any Spanish impetus, religious or legal. They were projects carried out beyond the purview of the Spaniards, in the hopes of preserving the knowledge and perspectives of the ancestors. There are fifteen such texts, from a variety of central Mexican towns (see Table 1).

In this book, many of the stories from these sources are summarized or quoted. In each case, if the story was taken directly from the original manuscript, the citation is to a folio in that original. (Curious readers do not have to go to a foreign research library to find out more! They will find a list of published versions in the bibliography.) Likewise, if a story was taken from a trusted published translation, the citation is to a page in that volume.

There are two other kinds of sources that are also included. The first set is the poetic song lyrics that were transcribed in Tenochtitlan (Mexico City) in the 1560s and 1570s, now called the "Cantares Mexicanos." The project seems to have been suggested by a friar, as the Aztecs were not in the habit of writing such things down; they simply remembered their songs. Beyond that initial impetus, however, the surviving texts are very much Nahua productions.

Common Name of the Text	Communities of Origin
Codex Aubin	Mexico (Tenochca people)
Bancroft Dialogues	Texcoco
Codex Chimalpahin	Chalco, Mexico, Texcoco
Chimalpahin's Eight Relations	Chalco, Mexico
Annals of Cuauhtitlan	Cuauhtitlan
Annals of Juan Bautista	Mexico (Tenochca)
Legend of the Suns	Mexico
Libro de Guardianes	Cuauhtinchan
Annals of Puebla	Puebla-Tlaxcala Valley
Annals of Tecamachalco	Tecamachalco
Hernando Alvarado Tezozomoc [within Codex Chimalpahin]	Mexico
Annals of Tlatelolco	Mexico (Tlatelolca people)
Annals of Tlaxcala	Puebla-Tlaxcala Valley
Historia Tolteca Chichimeca	Cuauhtinchan
Juan Buenaventura Zapata y Mendoza	Tlaxcala

Table 1 Sources of Aztec Stories

For generations, the Nahuas had been in the habit of repurposing old songs for new contexts. In the annals, they tell us quite frankly that they merely changed the name of a king or a god or a mountain and then used an old song anew. Because in the colonial era they sometimes replaced old gods' names with "Jesús" or "Malia" (Maria, for the Virgin Mary), scholars who do not read Nahuatl

The 16th-century author of the Codex Aubin took a pre-conquest-style timeline and placed next to it Nahuatl sentences resembling what an oral performer would have said in the old days.

have sometimes insisted that these productions are more Christian than Aztec. But nothing could be further from the truth: the style, the metaphors, the grammar—all indicate that the genre was very old and completely foreign to European traditions.[5]

The second additional set of sources is a mid-sixteenth-century encyclopedia-like work orchestrated by the Franciscan friar Bernardino de Sahagún that has come to be known as the "Florentine Codex" because the original resides in Florence, Italy. It has long been the single most relied-upon source in nearly all studies of the Aztecs. On one hand, this makes sense, as the friars asked Indigenous aides to interview scores of elders and to write down what they said about the old life. On the other hand, the source is problematic, as the Spaniards had arranged for leading questions to be posed, particularly about the evil nature of the old gods and ceremonies. This book quotes the Florentine Codex when it offers rich and detailed Nahuatl-language expression that does not seem to have been produced in response to direct questions, but rather, to have flowed freely and voluntarily. The Florentine Codex is, in short, most useful to us when its utterances include what the Spaniards would least have expected or wanted to hear, for these sections are more likely to represent the words of someone speaking unselfconsciously and from the heart.

What are *excluded* from this book are Spanish-language sources. This is, of course, a judgment call. Not all such texts were written with venom or derision, like Bernal Díaz's comment about the Aztecs feeding prisoners of war to gigantic pet snakes. Some were written by reasonable and thoughtful European men, a few of whom had even been raised from childhood among the Nahuas and spoke the language. Certain other Spanish-language sources were written by mixed-heritage descendants of Indigenous people, who themselves had some knowledge about the old ways, gleaned from talking to elders or studying the old glyphs. Yet this book will set all their testimony aside, for once we start down the path of allowing evidence from people who were not raised in the traditions and often had very limited knowledge of them, we can find ourselves in strange and doubtful territory. Probably someday, after more attention has been dedicated to the purely Nahuatl sources, it will be the right moment to return to these other, more removed sources to make comparisons and consider what they might teach us. But for a while, it is time we stopped relying on them.

In keeping with the Thames & Hudson series, this book uses the term "myth," but it does so cautiously. The word "myth" can refer to any foundational tale, often of a spiritual nature; but it can also refer to a story that is false. When we use this European term to describe the religious stories of regions or traditions that were once conquered or partially suppressed by Europeans, we run the risk of seeming to indicate that the stories of that region or tradition are somehow lesser, or wrongheaded. A reference to "Aztec myths" is thus potentially insulting, in a way that references to "Celtic myths" or "Greek myths" are not. This book therefore most often speaks of Aztec "stories," but it does not avoid the word "myth" entirely. After all, the term conveys a sense of the importance of particular, foundational stories in a way that no other word does. It invites us into a spiritual world that many of us want to know more about. The Aztec bards certainly would not have worried about the use of a particular foreign word. They would have been more interested in ushering us into the circle of expectant listeners sitting around an evening fire, waiting for them to begin their tale.

2

~~~~~

THE DIVINE UNIVERSE

It is told that when all was yet in darkness, when yet
no sun had shone and no dawn had broken—it is said—
the gods gathered together and took counsel among
themselves.

…When midnight had come, all the gods encircled
the hearth, called *teotexcalli*, where for four days fire
had burned.

…Nanahuatzin, daring all at once, resolved himself
[to create the sun]. He hardened his heart, and shut his
eyes firmly. He did not frighten himself over it. He did
not stop short; he did not falter; he did not turn back.
All at once he threw himself into the fire.[1]

In the beginning, there was time. The years stretched backward
into the primordial, formless past, and forward indefinitely into
the future yet to be imagined. For the Aztecs, people became
civilized—that is, demonstrated that they understood their place
in the wider universe—when they began to track and record the
passage of time. For them, the equivalent of a century consisted of
four sets of thirteen solar years. Whenever they officially founded a
new city-state, they would "bundle" a group of fifty-two years that
had just passed, and celebrate the occasion of the founding by making
a written record of its position in time relative to the bundling of

The Aztec Sun Stone, also called the Aztec Calendar Stone, shows the twenty day signs. Twelve feet in diameter and weighing about twenty-five tons, the piece was carved not long before the conquest. Art historians still debate its purpose. The Spaniards buried the stone under Mexico City's main town plaza, and it was not rediscovered until 1790.

the years. And they kept those records going. At the same time, they maintained a separate, regularly repeating ceremonial calendar of 260 days. Centuries later, long after the Spanish conquest, many of them still remembered how to track and record time in the old ways.

The Aztec Calendar

Like almost all other ancient Mesoamericans, the Aztecs were always measuring time in two ways: At any one moment, they knew where they were in a solar-based annual calendar, and they could also locate themselves in a complex repeating cycle of spiritual day names. (In our own way, in the Anglophone tradition, we do much the same thing: we are aware of the date, and we also keep track of an unrelated repeating list of days that are named for Nordic gods.)

The oldest Mesoamerican calendar was the cycle of spiritual day names. Twenty repeating day signs were lined up with the numbers one through thirteen, also repeating, creating 260 unique pairings of a name and a number before the cycle began again. It is thought that this count was probably invented by midwives, calculating from the first day of a missed menstrual period to the day of birth, which is generally very close to 260 days. Babies were supposed to be named for the day on which they appeared. Although the twenty signs and their referents varied somewhat throughout Mesoamerica, they were on a deep level very similar. Table 2 (opposite) lists the images and names as they existed among the Aztecs.

Meanwhile, the solar calendar was also running: eighteen months of twenty days each yielded a total of 360 days, followed by a period of five blank, frightening days (the *nemontli*, "those which belonged nowhere"), during which people prayed daily in the darkness before the dawn, waiting for the sun to rise in the east.

The two cycles of time both returned together to the point at which they had started every fifty-two years, so time was ceremonially "bundled" and marked at that point, in much the same way as we note the passing of an old century and the start of a new one.

Each solar year was given the name of the 260-day cycle figure that appeared as the last day of the last (or eighteenth) month, which always worked out to be Reed, Flint Knife, House, or Rabbit. In another tie to the ceremonial calendar, these four year signs repeated in groups of thirteen, yielding a total of fifty-two possible year names. So they would see the years One Reed, Two Flint Knife, Three House, Four

Symbol	Nahuatl Name / English Translation	Symbol	Nahuatl Name / English Translation	Symbol	Nahuatl Name / English Translation
	Cipactli / Alligator		Tochtli / Rabbit		Cuauhtli / Eagle
	Ehecatl / Wind		Atl / Water		Cozcacuauhtli / Vulture
	Calli / House		Itzcuintli / Dog		Olin / Motion/Quake
	Cuetzpallin / Iguana		Ozomatli / Monkey		Tecpatl / Flint Knife
	Coatl / Snake		Malinalli / Grass		Quiahuitl / Rain
	Miquiztli / Death		Acatl / Reed		Xochitl / Flower
	Mazatl / Deer		Ocelotl / Ocelot		

Table 2 The Aztec Day Signs

Rabbit, Five Reed, Six Flint Knife, Seven House, Eight Rabbit, Nine Reed, Ten Flint Knife, Eleven House, Twelve Rabbit, Thirteen Reed; to be followed by One Flint Knife, Two House, and so on.

How much each individual on the street knew about this system is debated. Some people may have been aware of only part of the calendar. But the priests, doctors and soothsayers certainly knew it all. They could count time in ways so complex that today we find it hard to follow.

CREATING THE WORLD

In the long unfolding of time, there had been several disastrous endings, but new life had always arisen. Indeed, there had been four suns before the current one: Four times in the past the world had seen destruction, followed by a new beginning. Individual storytellers remembered the order of events and some of the details differently, but the gist remained the same.[2] One of the suns—perhaps the first, or perhaps the most recent, had been born on the day Four Water; eventually, the sun died and the people were swept away by floods and turned into fish. Another sun was born on the day Four Wind. The people were later turned to monkeys and blown through the branches of the trees around the earth. Another sun was born on the day Four Ocelot. That era's people had been eaten by giant felines or other man-eaters—or perhaps it was the sun itself that had been eaten, swallowed in an eclipse from which there was no recovery. (To describe an eclipse of the sun, the Aztecs always said, "The sun was eaten," and in fact it did look rather like a tortilla or a cookie with a bite taken out of it.) It was definitely the third sun that had been born on the day Four Rain, but the fates had not been alluding to a watery rain, but rather, to a rain of fire, the lava burying the people of that time in a single day. This story may have been born from an ancient communal memory of the volcanic destruction of the great city-state of Cuicuilco, in about the year 200. Or perhaps the storytellers were simply completing a litany of destructive divine acts, each making possible a new creation.

Now the people lived under the Fifth Sun, born on the day Four Movement (*Nahui Olin*), the root word *olini* implying the possibility of the danger of great earthquakes (a constant threat in their

With their love for the sun and the moon, 16th-century Indigenous artists rapidly adopted European conventions in their portrayal of the two and then made creative adaptations.

land). The story of the creation of the Fifth Sun was very beautiful. "When all was yet in darkness, when yet no sun had shone and no dawn had broken—it is said—the gods gathered together and took counsel among themselves at Teotihuacan."[3] Teotihuacan was—and is—the site of the most impressive remains of ancient Mexico. Scholars don't know what language they spoke there, but the Aztecs, when they arrived from the north, were so awed by the remnants of the place that they named it in their own language "Place of Those Who Had Great Gods," or else "Place of People Who Become Gods," depending on how one heard the word.[4] In the story they told, the gods called for someone to be willing to do what was necessary. "Who will carry the burden? Who will take it upon himself to be the sun, to bring the dawn?" One who was very pleased with himself answered quickly. This was Tecuhciztecatl (Tekw-seez-TEK-at).

"Who else?" asked the gods. But no one else spoke up. One who did *not* step forth was Nanahuatzin (Na-na-WAH-tzeen), whose name meant "Pimply Faced." He just stood in the crowd listening to what was being said. But then the gods looked at him and said, "You will be the one, Nanahuatzin." Even though he had not asked for it, he accepted the task that was handed to him, acknowledging, "You have been good to me, o gods."

So for four days both Tecuhciztecatl and Nanahuatzin did penance and prepared themselves for a holy task. At midnight the gods dressed them, giving a heron-feather headdress to Tecuhciztecatl, who had been first to volunteer himself, but only a paper crown to Nanahuatzin. Then it was time. Tecuhciztecatl again went first. "He went to cast himself into the fire. And when the heat reached him, it was insufferable, intolerable, unbearable.… He became terrified, stopped in fear, turned about, and went back. Then once more he set out." Four times he tried. "But he could in no way dare to do it."

Next it was the turn of Nanahuatzin, who had never before thought of himself as a hero. "He hardened his heart, and shut his eyes firmly. He did not frighten himself over it. He did not stop short; he did not falter; he did not turn back. All at once he threw himself into the fire. He burned; his body crackled and sizzled." (Afterwards, seeing what Nanahuatzin had done, Tecuhciztecatl did throw himself in and he became the moon, but the glory was never to be his. He would never shine as bright.) The gods waited to see what would happen, looking in all directions, for they didn't know where the sun would appear. "And when the sun came to rise, when he burst forth, he appeared red. He kept swaying from side to side. It was impossible to look into his face; he was blinding."[5] Once again, new life, a glorious new life, had followed death, as light had followed darkness.

UNDERSTANDING DIVINITY

Nanahuatzin's quiet courage was richly rewarded. The world of the Fifth Sun was stunningly beautiful, profoundly moving. Like the moon, the eagle and the jaguar had leapt into the flames after Nanahuatzin, demonstrating that they were courageous in the way of warriors, who likewise would risk all for the sake of their people:

> It is told how there flew up an eagle, who was following
> the other beings [who were trying to create a sun]. It threw
> itself suddenly into the bonfire. It cast itself in while the
> fire still blazed up. So it is that its feathers are scorched-
> looking and blackened. Afterwards followed a jaguar.
> He came to fall in when the fire no longer burned high.
> He was just burned in various places, singed by the fire,

In each ceremonial month, the Aztec worshippers dressed as different divine figures who could be interpreted in varying ways. After the conquest, some said this one, from the Codex Telleriano-Remensis, was Tezcatlipoca, some Huitzilopochtli.

Book 11 of the Florentine Codex represents all aspects of the natural world. The artists showed both their love of naturalistic detail and their creative imagination. In the divine universe they knew, a flying fish might be revealed as resembling a bird, or a bee might be the star of a great drama. A snake might attack from underground on an otherwise gorgeous day, or a feathered serpent might suddenly seem to hover in the sky.

for it was no longer burning so hot. So it is that he was
only spotted, dotted with black spots, as if splashed with
black. From this, it is said, they took—from here was
taken—the custom of calling and naming one who
was valiant, a man [that is, a true warrior]: He was
given the name eagle-jaguar.

When eagles soared and jaguars screamed it was heart-stirring.
Poets raised their voices to honor the moment: "The eagle was
calling, the jaguar cried. And you, a red flamingo, went flying onward,
from the midst of a field to a place unknown."[6]
Truly, all the earth stirred the heart, everywhere one looked.
Blue-green waters flowed, rainbows shimmered, fish glistened, birds
darted, flowers gloried in their loveliness: "I hear the flower songs,
as if the hills were singing back to them."[7] In fact, all the earth was
imbued with the quality of the divine, if one could but see it. And
these most courageous of animals or beautiful of earthly delights
helped ordinary people to see it. It was the job of artists, musicians
and sometimes storytellers to render this divinity visible, and so
they often focused on such imagery as they went about their work.
In western myths, there is generally a strong element of dualism,
of good versus evil, light versus dark, and so on. But the Aztec philosophy exemplifies monism. In the words of an anthropologist who
has worked for decades with living Nahuatl speakers: "Monism ... [is]
a world view in which people regard every living being, inanimate
object, and natural process as an expression of one single substrate
or ground of existence. This substance, energy, or essential quality is
all powerful, sacred, and omnipresent, even though it remains largely
invisible and thus difficult for people to discern in their daily lives."[8]

In their songs, the Aztecs often referred to Ipalnemoani (Ee-pal-ne-mo-WA-nee), "That by Which There Is Life," or Tloque Nahuaque (TLO-kay Na-WA-kay), "That Which Is Close, That Which Is Near" [surrounds me on all sides]. They seemed to be speaking of a divine principle that connected all humans with all of nature.

According to this interpretation—and contrary to what westerners have often wanted to believe—the Aztecs were not really polytheistic. Rather, they were pantheistic. Divinity was everywhere, revealing itself to humans in the guise of virtually infinite divine beings, who were all aspects of the same force. Scholars who have expected to find a clear-cut pantheon, comparable to the Olympian gods of ancient Greece, for instance, have often been frustrated, for the gods' names and attributes seem to multiply and overlap with others, so that it is almost impossible to determine which figure was the god of what aspect of life. Instead, the face of god might suddenly reveal itself in the corn one was cooking (she should be treated kindly) or a precious stone a fisherman found in the belly of a pelican (who was, after all, the "king of water birds," and the "heart of the water"[9]), or likewise in a rushing river, or a shooting star, or a rainbow. Sometimes even a wind had a holy name. And each and every person giving these entities names or seeing the divine in them might envision the situation somewhat differently.

Certainly every single small ethnic state, or *altepetl* (al-TE-pet, literally, "water-mountain," the prerequisites for founding a village), had its own protector god or force, whose characteristics could shift. The people gave a name to an emanation of the divine with whom they could speak, and in their stories they gave the same name to the priests who helped them pray to the divine, who helped them extract answers to their questions or solutions to their problems from the tutelary god. As they traveled, these priests carried sacred bundles, filled with objects that revealed, or embodied in a visible form, the divinity of the universe: precious gems and shells, silken feathers, aromatic fir leaves. The priests buried the bundles at the base of their temples whenever they established them, hoping they would help them to call out to the divine. In the case of the Mexica, the name of their protector god was Huitzilopochtli (Wee-tzeel-o-POCH-tlee, "Left-footed like a Hummingbird"); his temple, and the prayers addressed to him, changed markedly over the years.

Occasionally the sources reveal very directly the fluidity in the situation. One elder, in telling a story, said that a certain people had always worshipped Mixcoatl (Meesh-CO-wat, sometimes glossed as the god of the hunt), but when they joined forces with another group, they happily agreed to rename him Citecatl (See-TEK-at) (a more feminine being), the name of the more powerful group's protector god.[10] The name was only a label, after all, designed to help humans. In a comparable vein, when an Indigenous aide later explained to the Spanish friars how midwives had delivered babies, he quoted the women as calling out to a variety of gods, finally exclaiming, "Who even knows the ones to whom they called."[11]

Nevertheless, the mosaic of divine qualities did regularly arrange themselves in the personas of three gods, or one might say three great principles, whom everyone recognized, though they did not always see them in exactly the same way. The three principles were: chaos (or unpredictable change); the earthly world (both lush and dry) upon which all humans depended; and an ethereal, almost ineffable creative force transgressing boundaries and bringing beauty to humans' lives.

The first of these three principles or forces was recognized as the greatest or most powerful. This was Tezcatlipoca, "Smoking Mirror,"

The *Altepetl*

The Aztecs valued both sovereignty and connectedness. They organized their lives according to what one scholar has called a "cellular principle."[12] Small political entities joined together to form a larger unit, and these larger units could in turn band together to form a yet larger entity. At each level, people enjoyed a measure of self-governance, but they were also invested in being part of a larger community and accepted that compromise was necessary.

The most important unit was the *altepetl*, generally understood to be a small city-state mostly inhabited by people of the same ethnicity. The term literally meant "water-mountain" and undoubtedly alluded to the idea that every settlement needed a defensible position as well as a water source. But the term also had deep spiritual associations. Towns that were by no means on a hilltop still used the universally recognized glyph that showed a hill rising above a watery cave, an allusion to life born of earth and water, and to the mysteries of the inner earth. ("They used to say that the hills were just magical, with earth, with rock on the surface; that they were just like jars or chests; that they were filled with the water which was there."[13]) Every place recognized as an altepetl had its own *tlatoani*, literally "speaker," a reference to the idea that a leader spoke on behalf of the entire group. (In English we translate this word as "chief" or "king.")

Every altepetl was composed of smaller units. Sometimes these were called *calpolli* (meaning "big house"), sometimes *tlaxilacalli* (a house of some kind, though the literal meaning is lost to us). Each of these subunits was governed by a *teuctli*, a dynastic overlord, and all the people who were related to him were considered to be *pilli* (plural: *pipiltin*), or nobles. In times of crisis, one of these dynastic overlords might challenge the tlatoani of the whole altepetl. Normally, however, things went along peacefully, with the various calpolli cooperating by sharing tasks between them. It might be one unit's job to repair the temple this year, for instance, and another unit's the next year; we might think of each calpolli as a combined parish and ward but with a nobleman at its head.

Likewise, multiple small altepetls might band together to form a *huey altepetl*, or "greater altepetl." In that case, each unit, or *tlayacatl* (called a sub-altepetl in English, or a *parcialidad* in Spanish), had its own independent tlatoani, but by working towards consensus they were able to act as a unified conglomerate in their dealings with outsiders. These entities, in fact, could be as large as participants cared to imagine: under colonial Spanish rule, the Nahuas would sometimes refer to all of Mexico as their "altepetl"!

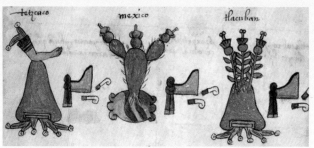

The glyph meaning "altepetl" always contained a pyramid-shaped mountain with the sign for water buried at its feet. A town's specific name would appear above. The only exception was the sign for the Aztec capital of *Tenochtitlan* (below, center): a stone (*-te-*) served as a platform for a cactus bearing the prickly-pear *nopalli* fruit (*-noch-*), sometimes followed by the sign for "at the place of" (*-titlan*).

the name referencing the mysterious depths and motion seen in reflections (especially in obsidian mirrors). He was the bringer of change through conflict or random acts of power. Often he was called by other names: Titlacahuan ("We Are His Servants"); Moyocoya ("Creator"); Moquequeloa ("Mocker"); Necoc Yaotzin ("War on Both Sides"); Yohualli ("Night," sometimes "Night Wind"); or Teixmatini ("Knower of Others"). Once in a while people said he himself was simply Ipalnemoani. Tezcatlipoca brought joy to all mortals, riches to merchants, and power to chiefs. But he could as easily take these things away again. Sometimes he punished people who were faithless or arrogant, but sometimes he capriciously brought loss even to those who had done nothing wrong. Then the people cried out to him, begging for mercy, desperate that he not mock them, that he not destroy them, as easily as they might smash a gemstone, or crush a feather. At a funeral, they might sing, "The jade breaks into pieces, the feather splits. You laugh. We are nothing: you look

The god of the hunt, Mixcoatl, holds arrows and a pouch of food. He was closely associated with both Tezcatlipoca and the earth divinities, like Tlalteuctli, a partner of Tlaloc.

upon us as nothing. You hide us, destroy us [kill us]."[14] Tezcatlipoca could do whatever he wanted.

The second divine figure or principle whom everyone recognized was most often called Tlaloc ("Covered with Earth" or "Filled with Earth"). Sometimes he was called Xoxouhqui ("Green One"), or Tlamacazqui ("Giver"). The Spaniards called him the god of rain—but matters were not really so simple. He appeared also as various Tlaloque (plural of Tlaloc), one of whom lived in every mountain, and one in every spring. And the Tlaloque were found elsewhere: Atlacoya ("Drainer of Waters") could prevent drought. Napa Teuctli ("Lord of the Four Directions") could suddenly be said to be one of the Tlaloque because he made reeds grow in the lake where the Mexica lived. The Tlaloque's figurative "elder sister," their leading lady, was Chicome Coatl ("Seven Snake"), sometimes called Cinteotl ("Divine Corn"), who helped crops grow. Tlaloc could torment or offer mercy to Tlalteuctli ("Earth Lord"), understood to be female sometimes, male at other times. Some said Tlaloc had a consort or a sister, Chalchiuhtlicue ("Jade Green Skirt"), while others said that she, too, was one of the Tlaloque. She lived in waves and rushing water and could overturn a canoe—but often she was the rain itself, another way of understanding Tlaloc. When the people prayed for rain, they might supplicate any or all of these beings, sometimes addressing them as "Master," and calling out to them almost exactly as they did to Tezcatlipoca, begging for mercy. These prayers reminded the gods that ordinary folk did not deserve to suffer drought:

> Here are the common folk, those who are the tail and wings [of society]. They are perishing. Their eyelids are swelling, their mouths drying out. … Thin are their lips and

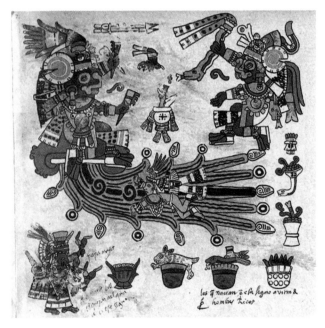

A representation of Tlaloc in the Codex Borbonicus.

blanched are their throats. With pallid eyes live the babies, the children [down to the youngest]—those who totter, those who crawl, those who spend their time turning dirt and potsherds, those who live sitting on the ground, those who lie on the boards, who fill the cradles. All the people face torment, affliction. They witness that which makes humans suffer. There are none who are passed over.[15]

Of the three best known divine figures or principles, the hardest to define was Quetzalcoatl ("Feathered Snake," or, more literally,

"Snake like a Quetzal Bird"). He could move from earth to sky, and as a crosser of boundaries was the protector of priests. He was in the wind and in storms (though Tezcatlipoca also could be there), giving him the epithet "road sweeper for the Tlaloque." Most importantly, and hardest to put into words, he brought with him zest and creativity, a quality of reaching for something greater than what was immediately before one. He was associated with the finest artistry and craftsmanship. In one story, it was Quetzalcoatl who first made humans out of ash—or maybe it was from the bones from prior ages—and then obtained corn for them to eat. Always he was associated with creation and birth, even called Teyocoani ("Creator of People"), and in prayers was often paired with Cihuacoatl Quilaztli, "Woman Snake," a brave warrior goddess often called upon by midwives. Yet this creative force also could be harsh. He was associated

Carvings of Chalchiuhtlicue are found throughout central Mexico.

The feathered serpent as represented in the Codex Borgia.
Note that even he is allowing himself to be sacrificed.

with Venus, the morning star, and on certain days when Venus rose, brought death to certain groups of people. (It might be the turn of the very old, for instance, or on other days, of the very young.) The creator, it seemed, could also be the destroyer.

Thus we return to the idea that the characteristics of the gods circled in upon each other and in some ways were always one. When midwives called out to Quetzalcoatl Teyocoani and Cihuacoatl Quilaztli, they also chanted that the new birth had been spoken of, or ordained, by the Two (Ome Teuctli, "Two Lord," and his consort, Ome Cihuatl, "Two Woman"), alluding to a dyad of fates who seem to have lived in the upper layers of the universe.[16] Likewise, when Quetzalcoatl had initially sought materials to make humanity, he had gone to Mictlan, the land of the dead deep in the earth, to seek the bones of beings of prior eras; and he begged for what he needed from a male–female dyad, this time Mictlan Teuctli ("Lord of the Land of the Dead") and Mictecacihuatl ("Lady of the Dead People"), who consented and gave him verbal instructions.[17] These were not just parallel stories; they were in some senses the same story. The words of male and female, uttered together, brought life.

TELLING STORIES OF THE GODS

All the dozens—even hundreds—of overlapping gods could appear as characters in stories of ancient times. In that context, they were god-beings who walked the earth, participating in human-like dramas, but with cosmic significance. Some storytellers, on the other hand, believed that they were speaking of ancient human beings, mere mortals named for the gods they served, who had absorbed some of the power of the divine. We see their different perceptions of the situation in the stories they left us. The same beings and even narratives could take different forms. One storyteller might envision a capricious natural world, a divinity whom humans needed to learn to handle, while another might speak of basic human emotions, a world of ingratitude and revenge, desire and appeasement, albeit on a divine stage. Consider, for instance, the story of the powerful goddess Itzpapalotl ("Obsidian Butterfly"). She gave early humans directions as to how to shoot the arrows she had gifted to them—instructions that one cannot help noting were reflective of the Aztecs' experiences in migrating south as warlike bands in search of fabled green valleys: "You must go to the east, and there you must shoot. Likewise to the north, to the desert lands, and there you must shoot. Likewise to the west, and there you must shoot. Likewise to the garden lands, the flower lands, and there you must shoot."[18]

In one version of the story, when the roving people of the arrow came along shooting, the four hundred Mixcoa ("Cloud Snake

Sacred Bundles

Throughout the Native American world, a wide variety of peoples maintained and protected sacred bundles. These bundles contained treasured items that embodied divinity, that revealed divinity to ordinary mortals. Sometimes they held bones of ancestors, sometimes light-reflecting minerals, such as mica, or other beautiful elements of the natural world.

Ancient Mesoamerican art of both the Mayan and central Mexican worlds depicts such bundles as being rounded, with elaborate knots. Sacred bundles also appear in the oldest Aztec stories, which tell of priests who carried the bundles for their people in their ongoing migrations, protecting them carefully. When they settled down, they spoke of burying a bundle or bundles beneath their temple, at its "heart," as they said.

Not all bundles were old. They were created when people faced special circumstances. In one story, the Mexica asked the king of Culhuacan, who was allowing them to settle on his land, to bless their endeavor by giving them another sacred bundle: "'Now, lord, give us a little something for the heart of our earthen altar.' Then the *tlatoani* said, 'Very good. You deserve it. May the priests give it a heart.'" But in an effort to destroy the Mexica, whom he feared, the king decided to give them a dangerous bundle that embodied the worst aspects of the universe, filth and disorder. "He gave orders

People") were in the lead, and despite the fact that they were doing her bidding, the uncaring goddess felled them and ate them all up. All but one, that is: The youngest, simply called Mixcoatl, escaped. He hid inside a helpful desert cactus, then leapt out and killed Itzpapalotl. He turned her ashes into a sacred bundle to embody her divinity forever, and for years it protected the people. Indeed, one early chief's widow who became ruler in her own right, named Xiuhtlacuilolxochitzin

The four bearers of the Aztecs' sacred bundles, as represented in the early post-conquest Codex Boturini. There were three men and one woman.

to the priests, saying to them, 'Give them a heart of excrement and hair, and also a *poxaquatl* [a bird that flies erratically].' The priests went to place the heart at night [in secret]." Fortunately, the Mexica priests had the sense to look inside the sacred bundle that had been gifted to them. "They became really sad." Of course, they destroyed it and replaced it with a different bundle, one that contained especially beautiful and powerful leaves that were used in ceremonies.[19]

("Year Painter Flower") in honor of the painted histories she kept, was said to have her knowledge and talents precisely because she was so good at invoking the power of Itzpapalotl. In this rendition of the story of Itzpapalotl, life was hard, but perfectly manageable if one understood how to handle the divine.[20]

Another version of the story, however, was much more frightening, combining the various elements in an entirely different way

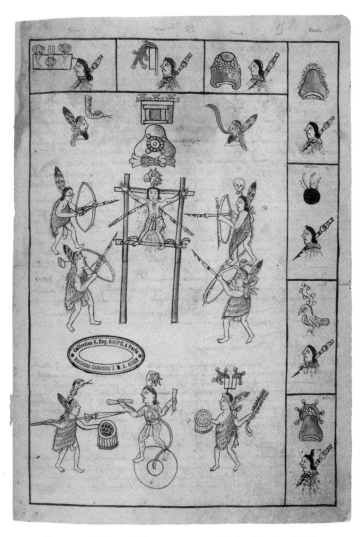

The Historia Tolteca Chichimeca was created a few decades after the conquest by people living in Cuauhtinchan, in the Tlaxcala valley. Bows and arrows play a central role in the drama.

so as to give vent to primal emotions. Here, the character called Mixcoatl was a god-being whose wife gave birth to four hundred children, but these were neither grateful nor dutiful. Mixcoatl—at one point so powerful that he is called "the sun"—even gave them birds so they could use the feathers to make darts and hunt and then give offerings to their father, but they did not. Instead they spent their time fornicating and drinking a lot of *pulque* (cactus wine). So Mixcoatl told his five youngest children (whom he liked the best) to destroy their siblings, and they did. A few, however, survived. One day, two of these went hunting for deer, spending all day and all night cruelly chasing down the vulnerable creatures. Then two of those who had once been deer transformed into women, and came to seduce the two hunters. One of the men fell for the ruse, and the woman turned on him in a rage and tore his heart out. The other brother got away, his feminine pursuer fortunately (for him) getting caught on a helpful desert cactus, and he came home crying for his dead sibling. He and the other Mixcoa decided to burn the figure they knew as Itzpapalotl, and turn her into a bundle to make her the people's spirit power. Then, newly empowered by a protector god, the Mixcoa man—now also called simply Mixcoatl—gave vent to his rage by going on a sort of rampage, a veritable conquering spree.

Eventually he came across Chimalman, the woman of his dreams. At a loss for what to do, he shot at her. When the first arrow came, she ducked. When the second came, she dodged to the side. When the third came, she caught it in her hand. When the fourth came, she let it pass between her legs. Then she turn and ran into a gorge, so that he could not find her. Mixcoatl's violence against others continued, so the woman's compatriots asked her to go to him. She consented, and she became pregnant with a god-being named

Pulque Traditions

The maguey (or agave) plant was highly valued by the Aztecs. Its thick, fleshy leaves can be fermented and turned into *pulque* (one variant of which is the drink we now call tequila). The skin of the leaves can be made into paper, and the fibers can be twisted into string, like hemp, which the Aztecs used to weave simple clothing when cotton was not readily available. The Aztecs made needles out of the thorns found on the leaves' edges, and when the perennial plant was eventually worn out, they boiled and ate the roots and turned the leaves into thatch for their roofs.

Yet despite their love of this extraordinary plant, the Aztecs were ambivalent about its primary product, pulque. Several stories tell of figures who drank to the point of excess, and in their drunkenness committed crimes against their societies. (Quetzalcoatl, for instance, forgot his priestly duties and slept with his own sister.) Indeed, only elderly people were considered to have earned the right to drink as much as they wanted to. So the Aztecs certainly did not want to conflate the miraculous maguey plant with pulque. Art historians have found that the pre-Columbians in general associated one goddess with maguey, and different divinities (usually male) with pulque. Among the Aztecs, the latter were the Four Hundred Rabbits, possibly representing the four hundred Huitznahua killed by Huitzilopochtli, or sometimes a collective divinity called Ome Tochtli, Two Rabbit, the spirit of a calendar day. "It was said that he who was born then would be a great drunkard." It was, a commentator added, describing such a man's behavior, "as if he had given himself to [pulque]."[21]

Quetzalcoatl. From this story of rage and pain would come a figure of great creativity.[22]

The story of Quetzalcoatl likewise comes in several forms, but in essence the versions convey similar messages.[23] All agree that brave

Chimalman gave birth to Quetzalcoatl. In the most detailed and most powerful rendition, however, Chimalman does not wish to tell her son who his father had been, and he and others surmise that she had swallowed a magic stone (a motif common to a number of Native American traditions, always in connection to a pregnancy that had not been wanted). The most human-like Quetzalcoatl of the stories built exquisite temples out of precious stones and iridescent feathers. He introduced hot chocolate and ceramics. But Tezcatlipoca brought discord into this lovely world. First he brought self-doubt: He brought a mirror to Quetzalcoatl, who for the first time saw that he himself was not beautiful, like the world he was making, but rather ugly. He was horrified to think his people would see him as he really was and swore he would never show himself again. So his servants made him a turquoise mask. Pleased, Quetzalcoatl went forth to see the people and lead sacred ceremonies—but now Tezcatlipoca arranged to have him lose his self-restraint: He offered Quetzalcoatl too much pulque. In his drunkenness, Quetzalcoatl called for his sister, and he lay with her and let his ceremonial duties lapse. When he realized what he had done, in the midst of his shame and pain, he decided to leave his people, and he traveled east to Tlapallan ("Place of Colors"), leaving distinct land formations as stomped toward the coast. When he got there, he bravely set himself on fire:

And they say as he burned, his ashes rose. And what appeared and what they saw were all the precious birds, rising into the sky. They saw roseate spoonbills, cotingas, trogons, herons, green parrots, scarlet macaws, white-fronted parrots, and all the other precious birds. And as soon as his ashes had been consumed, they saw the heart of a quetzal bird rising upward, and so they knew he had gone to the sky, had entered the sky. Old people used to say he was changed into the star [Venus] that appears at dawn. Thus they say it appeared when Quetzalcoatl died, and they called him Lord of the Dawn.[24]

In some versions of the story, the being called Quetzalcoatl is more violent than this one was, but always he is a profoundly creative force who nevertheless is also capable of bringing death and destruction.

For the Mexica specifically, a central story was that of Huitzilopochtli, their protector god. The two surviving lengthy Nahuatl narratives about him share key elements: A god-being engages in a bloody struggle with his sister (and in one version, also his mother) when she wrongs him. Yet in the end, when Huitzilopochtli has killed

Long called "Moctezuma's headdress," this piece may not really have belonged to the king at all. Like other Aztec treasure, it is made of feathers, precious shells and stones, and bits of gold.

The feathers of the quetzal bird and other tropical avians
figure prominently in Aztec stories and art.

his sister (or his mother) there is no sense that justice has been done, but rather, simply that the past is full of pain and rage that we humans have no choice but to digest in order to move forward.

In one version, the goddess Coatlicue ("Snake Skirted") was mother to the four hundred Huitznahua people (one of the seven original *calpolli* units, or clans, making up the Mexica people). One day Coatlicue found a feather and bundled it near her heart; it made her pregnant. This was another case of a missing dad: "No one stepped forth as the father." Coatlicue's other children were enraged, not wanting to welcome a half-sibling by some unknown father who might supplant them. Her daughter Coyolxauhqui ("Bell-Dressed"), who as the eldest was understood to be the bearer of heirs, decided to make war against her own mother, to kill her and the child within. The terrified mother grew calm only when the being inside her revealed himself to be an emanation of the protector god Huitzilopochtli. He said what such figures always do: "Do not fear, for I know what to do." Waiting until the attackers grew close, he burst forth as a fully born babe, indeed, already as a warrior (humorously painting himself

Huitzillin: The Hummingbird

The Aztecs loved hummingbirds. Despite their small size, hummingbirds are admirably strong and skilled at surviving. They can fly at spectacular speeds or hover for long moments at any angle, even upside down. They can appear ferocious with their elegant, sword-like beaks, which they use to feed off of the nectar in flowers—which to the Aztecs were a symbol of warriors. To budget energy, hummingbirds can enter a state of torpor, almost appearing to be dead, then come to vivid life when conditions suit. Most of them live locally, but a few species

Varieties of hummingbirds as found in the Florentine Codex.

up with what he found in his dirty diaper!). Huitzilopochtli's rage in defense of his mother and himself knew no limits: "He pierced [his sister] Coyolxauhqui, and then he quickly struck off her head. It came to rest on the slope of Coatepetl ('Snake Mountain'). And her body went falling below; it went crashing in pieces; in various places her arms, her legs, and her body kept falling." Then the enraged baby-warrior went after his elder half-brothers, who had been on Coyolxauhqui's side. They pleaded with him, "but Huitzilopochtli did not calm his heart." Only a very few escaped him.[25]

migrate from the far north down into Mexico, along the very path that the ancestors of the Aztecs followed. In the sunlight, their bright-colored, iridescent feathers are stunningly beautiful.[26]

The Mexica in particular seemed to regard the hummingbird as a sort of alter-ego. Their tutelary god was named Huitzilopochtli. Despite the popular idea that the name meant "Hummingbird on the Left," it actually translates as "Left-footed [or Left-handed] like a Hummingbird." To the Nahuas, those who were left-handed were special and admirable; there was no stain attached to the trait as there was in western mythology. And to be like a hummingbird was of all things desirable for a warrior and leader of warriors. The god Huitzilopochtli was, as the stories show, a fighter, and he guided people who were survivors, too.

The Mexica said that an early leader of theirs, one who lived even before they constituted an *altepetl*, while they were still wanderers, was named Huitzilihuitl, which means "Hummingbird Feather." Perhaps they meant he was an offshoot of the god Huitzilopochtli; perhaps they simply meant he himself was reminiscent of a hummingbird; or perhaps they were alluding to the precious qualities of feathers. Probably all of these were true at once. For generations, some Mexica royal family members bore this ancestral name.

In another version, Huitzilopochtli more closely resembles a human priest acting in the name of the god, but the uncontrolled rage and its painful consequences remain the same. This time, Huitzilopochtli was leader of his people, and he decided that his sister, Malinalxochitl ("Twisted Grass Flower")—who was called the people's "elder sister," again meaning that they expected her to mother the heir—was up to no good. He did not like the fact that she was a powerful sorceress who used magic for bad purposes, "causing others to lose their way." So one day, when she was very pregnant and thus quite vulnerable, he led the people away while she slept. (Later, she would wake, and sob uncontrollably at being deserted.) Huitzilopochtli told the four hundred Huitznahua, "Her practice is not my practice." He said, "I have been given the arrow and the shield, for war is my practice, and by risking my breast and my head, I shall bring in the altepetls all around.… Not for nothing shall I conquer them. I shall bring into being the house of precious green stone, the house of gold, the house of precious quetzal feathers, the house of green jade, the house of spondylus shells, the house of amethysts." And much more wealth did he promise them. Ultimately Huitzilopochtli did a good job providing for the people, showing them all the edible creatures living in the lake in the middle of their valley. But they wanted more, reminding him that when he split up the group by leading some of them away from Malinalxochitl, he had promised them vast treasures. At this Huitzilopochtli became enraged—either at their ingratitude, or at the reminder of his own failings, or both. He killed the four hundred Huitznahua—beginning with his own mother, here named Coyolxauhcihuatl ("Bell-Dressed Woman"). Everyone was terrified; even the birds left the valley.[27]

Later, a sorcerer named Copil (a kind of crown), who was the child born to Huitzilopochtli's abandoned sister, came to find his uncle and fight with him. "Huitzilopochtli said, 'Good. Are you not the one my elder sister Malinalxoch gave birth to?'" (He truncated her name in order to insult his nephew.) "Then Copil said, 'Yes, it is I. I shall seize you; I am come to destroy you. Why did you leave my mother stealthily as she slept? I shall kill you!'" But in fact Huitzilopochtli killed him, too. He cut out Copil's heart, and told his people to throw it into the lake, in the midst of the reeds,

The discovery of this Aztec carving in 1978 eventually led to the excavation of the Templo Mayor. The stone's imagery clearly represents the story of Coyolxauhqui and her dismemberment.

where the city of Tenochtitlan would later be planted and grow to greatness. He told them they should stand on one of the peculiar rock formations left by the god Quetzalcoatl when he traveled east, and send the heart flying into the air in a certain direction. But—the storyteller added—although Copil died, Copil's daughter survived, and married a Mexica man and had descendants. So perhaps the past was not quite as grim as it first appeared.[28]

Most of the time, such storytellers were not trying to evoke the loveliness of the known universe: That was generally the job of the poets and singers. Rather, they were trying to help people think about sources of destructive discord and rage, and possible ways of handling such crises when they came, and of moving past them. They were far from being peaceniks: such an approach would have led their people to certain disaster in the world they knew. But they were also a long way from celebrating violence. They seemed to want people to understand the origins of violence, to see conflicts from multiple points of view. Scholars have sometimes thought that Huitzilopochtli's brutality toward his sister (or mother) bespeaks misogyny. But there is nothing in the sources to suggest that the storytellers or their audiences had imbibed a hatred of women. There was no relishing of what Huitzilopochtli did, and no sense that women needed to be put in their place as women. Listening to either version of the story, some would probably have been shocked and horrified by Huitzilopochtli's behavior; others would have thought he had no choice but to try to establish dominance, given the situations in which he found himself. It was, after all, strength that they wanted from a protector god. Yet even these would likely have had to acknowledge that his actions made them distinctly uncomfortable. (Remember, even the birds left!)

THE IDEA OF SACRIFICE

If there is one idea that all Aztec religious texts agree on, it is that people were expected to try to cherish the beauty, the specialness, the glory of this life on earth that we humans are given for a time. Storytellers and singers alike worked together to remind their audiences of all that they had to be grateful for. Time on earth was fleeting—they said it was "borrowed" from the universe—but it was all there was. So they should revel in it. They were not to waste what time they had, but rather, live life to the fullest: They were to treasure the people of their altepetl and work for their future. Mothers told their daughters on their marriages that although life was harder than it first seemed, it would nevertheless bring them great joy. They should remember that in the tough times, "For who," the mothers demanded, "is just yielding to death?"[29] When death came, it was final, but if people lived as they should, then their community would not die, and they themselves would be remembered with love. "I weep, I come suffering orphanhood," intoned the singers at a funeral. "I remember the jade, the greenery, the one whom we have burned, have shrouded."[30] They remembered the beloved dead as they were in life.

Aztec religious life centered on thanking the gods for the life that they had been given, at least for a little while. They did this in various ways—in collecting and spreading good-smelling fir, sweeping till floors were spotless, staying up all night in exhausting vigils, and in puncturing themselves with thorns and scattering their own blood. (Brave young men had to do this to their own penises!) But there was also the question of the need to give up human life to nourish the gods, in the same way that animals were asked to give themselves up to hunters that humans might live. Nanahuatzin had jumped into the fire to save his people, and Quetzalcoatl likewise had found the strength to do so when it seemed to him his people would be better off without him. Out of such trials, one had created the sun, and the other the morning star. But these were god-beings. Most humans could not bear to sacrifice their lives thus. Indeed, being too eager to give up the precious gift wouldn't have been right.

So it was that in the ancient stories, people preferred to offer up the lives of their enemies.

Throughout the Americas, it was widespread practice for an enemy warrior or two to be sacrificed after victory in battle. The doomed were not demeaned, but rather revered, especially if they died bravely. They were killed in a sacred space, amidst prayers. In Mesoamerica specifically, the practice of sacrificing an occasional prisoner of war had likewise existed for centuries. Traditionally, the victims were treated with great respect. And it was so among the Nahuatl-speaking Aztecs, too—at least at first. (Later, as we shall see, the Mexica leadership would weaponize the practice. They would come to kill substantial numbers every month. But they couldn't possibly afford to do so when their city-state was young and vulnerable. It would have been impossible, even unthinkable, at that stage.) Originally, those who were to die were housed in the lap of luxury and offered every kind of comfort. Those who were to

Sacred flint knives with mother-of-pearl eyes and teeth.

The pre-conquest Codex Borgia was not painted by the Mexica, but it does come from a closely related culture group in central Mexico. It served as a guide to priests in their sacrificial ceremonies. The complexity of their cosmovision is evident.

live understood themselves to be profoundly grateful to those who were to die. "He is like my son," intoned a captor when his battle-field captive was about to be slain.[31] Afterwards, the blood of the sacrificed person was taken to the homes of people in the calpolli, or neighborhood, that had offered him up, and it was brushed on the lips of clay figurines of whatever gods were worshipped there.[32] Thus the gods were fed.

Every person in central Mexico understood that death on a sacrificial stone could easily be their own fate if their people ever lost a war. They sang about that possibility, and told stories about it. They did not wish for it. In fact, there was an old saying, applied with sympathy to a person who was in some kind of serious trouble: "Already he is at the edge of the fire. Already he is at the temple stairway."[33] The commentator who wrote down the old adage added that it was naturally considered best to give useful warnings and advice *before* such a saying was truly apt.

The Aztecs did not think that they had to be willing to jump straight into the fire—for they showed themselves willing to risk death for their people in other ways. Young warriors were likened to flowers: They were gloriously beautiful specimens of the human frame, and at the same time as fragile as blossoms when they went off to war, risking death on the battlefield or the sacrificial pyre afterwards, if taken prisoner. Women risked their lives every time they went through childbirth: Quilaztli, the goddess whom they most often called to in their *miquizpan*, their time of facing death, carried a shield and helped them try to seize a life from the universe. If they died, they were considered holy, and powerful as well; indeed, women who had died giving birth were positively terrifying to most people who mentioned them.

There was, in fact, a bit more to the original creation story. The sun, who had once been plain old Nanahuatzin, found after he immolated himself that no matter how brightly he burned, he could not manage to move through the sky. Human beings came to his rescue: He was fed and carried by those who had been willing to die for their people. In the morning, warriors who had died in battle carried him to the zenith. In the afternoon, women who had died in childbirth carried him to his resting place. So it was that these two groups had indeed given up their lives for others, both concretely in the affairs of earth, and symbolically in their service to the sun.[34]

The Layered Universe

Within western scholarship, there has arisen a veritable mythology concerning the Aztecs' purported belief in nine or thirteen layers of sky, overseen by an omnipotent male/female duality in the uppermost layer, and an equivalent nine layers of the underworld. Unfortunately, no Nahuatl-language sources tell us this. The notion comes from somewhat discordant descriptions in two colonial sources, one a document written in Spanish by a Spaniard trying to make sense of what he had heard (the *Historia de los Mexicanos por sus pinturas*), and the other a set of annotated drawings created by an Italian (the Codex Vaticanus A, sometimes called the Codex Rios). The description in the latter certainly calls to mind Dante's *Divine Comedy*, which may well have been the inspiration.

However, there is some degree of truth to the story. Lyrics of ancient song-poems and certain annals do occasionally allude to the "nine layers" when they are speaking of the world, and there are also pre-conquest pictorial references to the notion of a great tree of life, with roots in the bowels of earth or in deep water and branches in the highest sky. Indeed, in many Indigenous North American religions we find trees acting as portals between worlds, so it would be remarkable if the Aztecs did *not* have such a concept. If only we could know more about it—but the Nahuatl sources tell us little on this subject. Probably each person had his or her own imaginative vision of such a tree, or at least of a layered world.

Later, Spanish friars assumed that Mictlan, the land of the dead, was synonymous with the underworld, or at least a certain layer of the underworld. But it wasn't always so. In Nahuatl-language sources, it sometimes referred to an airless cave at the depths of the world, but it also sometimes referred to the skies, where those who died in war traveled.

In this duty that they performed in the firmament, the young adults who had given up their earthly futures enjoyed an afterlife of sorts denied to others. For there were three possible fates upon death. A tiny few were taken to Tlalocan, a lush paradise without drought: These were people who had drowned or been struck by lightning, or who had died of illnesses related to rising water (tumors, swelling, blisters). Those who met such a fate were understood to have been particularly good at heart, and deserving of such a heaven.[35] Most people, however, traveled the dark road to Mictlan, the land of the dead, the "place of the end of the journey, the place of no outlet or opening.... You [the god] crush life like a feather. You erase it like a painting. All just go to Mictlan, our place of disappearing together."[36] People on earth who remembered those who had died prayed and sang for them for four years. But at the end of that time, the dead "completely disappeared."[37] Only those who went to feed and care for the sun in the sky lived on for a while in an aerial world inhabited by gorgeous birds and butterflies. There, they could enjoy the beauties of the world for a little bit longer. Indeed, some said they *were* the birds and butterflies. Most certainly, they were remembered and honored in song and prayer. But even they would eventually disappear. Time would move forward, and others would live in their place.

Over and over the myths made clear that accepting that reality was one of the conditions of finding joy in life, of appreciating what we have on earth for the time that it is given to us, for only change was eternal. But the pain of that inevitable loss could be softened by the knowledge that a person—or a people—would be remembered as time moved ever onward. And they would be remembered well if they lived honorably, fighting hard for life but accepting what could not be prevented—even death, whenever and however it came.

3

THE BEGINNINGS OF HUMAN SOCIETY

The [defeated] Mexica came to Culhuacan and established
themselves at Tizaapan. The Culhuaque said to them,
"Welcome, o Mexica. Settle there at Tizaapan." But when they
had been there ten days, the Culhuaque rulers gave them
an order, saying, "O Mexica, you must drag in a *chinampa*
[field], on which a crane will come to stand and a snake
who is discolored from sickness will come to lie. You are
to come place the chinampa outside the palace." After they
had come to give them the orders, the Mexica wept and said,
"Woe is us! How will we do it?" Then Huitzilopochtli spoke
to them and said, "Don't be afraid. I know how you are to
go and drag the chinampa that is over there. I will show
you." They were able to do it by dragging the sod in separate
pieces. The crane came along standing upon it, and the snake,
lively now, lay in the chinampa. The Culhuaque rulers were
amazed at it, saying, "Who *are* these Mexica!?"[1]

There was once a beautiful kingdom, in which all manner of people
got along well together. They raised their voices to give utterance
to song and story; they decorated their temples and homes with
gemstones, mother-of-pearl, and coral. *Chichimecs* (wild people)
with their bows and arrows had come down from the north and
intermarried with those born into this world of artistic genius.

Chichimecs

The Nahuas referred to people from the north whom they perceived as barbarians as "Chichimecs." A popular understanding has been that this meant "dog people," but that is not correct, as the word for dog (*chichi*) has two short "i" sounds, whereas the word "Chichimec" has two long "i" sounds (CHEE-CHEE-mec). In its earliest formation, the term is more likely to have referred to people who walked suckling their young, or whose upper bodies were uncovered (derived from the verb *chichi*, with two long "i" sounds, meaning "to suckle").

In any event, the colonial-era Nahuas used the term to refer to living people to the north (such as the Apache) as well as to their own ancestors, whom they fully understood to have been migrants from the desert country. In some ways, the Nahuas were condescending to Chichimecs when they spoke of them; but in other ways they betrayed a certain awe and admiration for the nomadic people's grit and style. This was true when the Nahuas spoke of their enemies to the north, whom they wished to portray as primitive and yet also feared; and it was equally true when they spoke of their forebears, whose savagery they mocked, but whose valor they were nonetheless proud of.

In their drawings of the Chichimecs, the Nahuas showed them wearing furs or stringy clothing made of maguey fibers rather than woven textiles. This idea made it into their stories, too. When an early Aztec *tlatoani* asked for a bride from among the long-settled, cotton-growing people of Cuernavaca, the king of Cuernavaca was supposed to have asked, "What will he give my daughter [to wear]? Perhaps he will clothe her with marsh plants and marsh plant thread, as he clothes himself ... !?"[2] That was his way of saying "No way!" to an upstart Chichimec who had sought to marry his daughter (see p. 105).

On the other hand, the Nahuas' drawings of the Chichimecs also always showed their impressive bows and arrows, with which they brought down enemies right and left. Their magical or nearly magical arrows made their way into stories, too, described

In the post-conquest Codex Azcatitlan, a Chichimec man,
wearing a shirt made of plant fibers, begins his long,
wandering path toward his new home.

as seeking a bird up in the sky, and, upon failing to find one,
zigzagging back to earth to bring down some other prey!

Chichimecs were understood to be not only hunters but also
warriors par excellence, and if there was a group of people whom
the Aztecs always admired, it was talented warriors. There was no
standing army: every boy was expected to grow up to participate
in war. Even priests and merchants did so in symbolic rituals.
Success in warfare could bring the most ordinary of young
men fame and wealth. He might even be named a *cuauhpilli*,
an eagle lord, meaning that he had achieved nobility not by birth
but through his deeds. No wonder the Nahuas were proud of
their "wild" ancestors.

The Nahuatl text accompanying this illustration in the Codex Azcatitlan describes the people's journey: "Here they were lost in the mountains, the forests, the rocky lands. The Mexica followed their path wherever it led."

In all the stories, the place they created together was called Tollan (rendered "Tula" in modern times). Literally, the name means "reedy place," and the central basin of Mexico where these people lived was indeed a swampland. But the name for its people, Tolteca—literally, "people of Tollan"—implied more: It was applied to any talented craftspeople or people of great accomplishment who had lived long ago. Yet despite the notion's prevalence as a motif, storytellers never devoted much time to life in Tollan. In the narratives they spun, it existed merely as a preliminary, an introduction to the time of discord and struggle that humans knew so well.

THE DISSOLUTION OF TOLLAN

For many years, scholars argued about whether Tollan (Tula) was or was not a real place. The archaeological remains near the town still called Tula in the state of Hidalgo (north of Mexico City) demonstrate that there once existed a powerful town on the site, so it was tempting to say that there lay the real Tollan. Yet the remnants at this site are not so dazzling as to be able to explain why nearly every Nahuatl-speaking group told tales of a utopian life in the city of the Toltecs. Nor does it make sense to think that every migrating group had once spent time in the exact same urban space.

What most scholars now agree is that Tollan was a symbolic name, representative of the varied agricultural peoples of central Mexico who accepted the migrants from the north into their midst. Their sedentary lifestyles had yielded pyramids, paintings, and irrigation projects that impressed the newcomers deeply, and thus became part of the stories they and their descendants told.

After brief allusions to a honeymoon period in Tollan, the story-tellers regularly got down to the business of describing the conflicts that eventually erupted. Events swirled around a political leader named Huemac ("Big Gift"), who was sent by the gods—sometimes from Tlaloc, sometimes from Tezcatlipoca. His name was something of a joke, for as gifts go, this one left much to be desired: Huemac was a troublemaker. He might demand a daughter of the chief of another group for sacrifice; he might make himself so unpleasant to others that his community's sorceresses demanded his *own* daughter be offered as a sacrifice; he might give his daughter as a bride to an outsider with egomaniacal tendencies. However it happened, he always managed to break the polity apart. In one version, Huemac killed himself when even his most loyal followers became so disgusted by his conduct that they would no longer follow him.[3]

By far the richest, most detailed version of the story was that told in Cuauhtinchan ("Home of the Eagles") in the Puebla-Tlaxcala valley, east of the central basin. The wild Chichimecs—here called the Tolteca Chichimeca—were living in Tollan with the relatively civilized Nonohualca, and were behaving rather badly. It wasn't really their fault. Tezcatlipoca had deceived them: he left a foundling for them to find and raise as their own. This was Huemac. The Chichimecs had no way of knowing he had been created to sow discord among them. They only knew he was a young prince.

When Huemac became a young man, he gave orders that
the Nonohualca tend to his home. The Nonohualca said
to him, "So be it, my lord. May we do what you desire."
The Nonohualca came to tend to his home. And then he
demanded women of them. He said to the Nonohualca,
"You are to give me women. I order that the buttocks be
four spans wide." The Nonohualca said to him, "So be it.
Let us seek where we can get one whose buttocks are four
spans wide." Then they brought four women who had not
yet known sexual pleasure. But as to size, they were not
enough. He said to the Nonohualca, "They are not of the
size I want. Their buttocks are not four spans wide. I want
them really big." The Nonohualca left in great anger.

Anyone listening to this story of a man's ridiculous demands had to
laugh, but as the narrative proceeded, matters grew more serious.
Huemac went on to do the most terrible, dishonorable thing one
could do to a conquered people's women: rather than maintaining
them as minor wives, as he had implied he would, he sacrificed them.
He tied the four new arrivals to an obsidian mirror table and left
them there to await their deaths. At this point, the Nonohualca had,
understandably, had quite enough. Equally understandably, they
blamed the Chichimecs—who had adopted Huemac—and made
war against them. Just as they were about to attain their coveted
victory, the Chichimecs begged them to desist. Their chief cried
aloud, "Was *I* the one who sent for the women over whom we are
fighting and making war? Let Huemac die! *He* made us fight!" The
two groups forged an alliance and together defeated Huemac, but in
an important sense, their new wisdom came too late. They had killed

too many of each other's sons. "The Nonohualca gathered together and talked. They said, 'Come, what kind of people are we? It seems we have done wrong. Perhaps because of it something may happen to our children and grandchildren. Let us go. Let us leave our lands.… We should leave." Fearing that they had failed in their human duty to try to get along with their kin, the Nonohualca did leave, and the rest of the story is an account of their efforts and those of the Chichimecs to find peace and stability without their former allies.

In the text, the Chichimecs become wanderers again, as they had been before they settled at Tollan—but nevertheless, they survive. Their chiefs lead them in prayer, at moments seemingly addressed to Tezcatlipoca, at moments to Quetzalcoatl, for in effect they are speaking to the divine universe. "Here he has placed us, our inventor, our creator. Will we have to hide our faces, our mouths [that is, will we have to die]? What does he say? How does he test us, our inventor, our creator, Ipalnemoani. He knows if we will be defeated. What will his heart order? O Tolteca, may you have confidence! Gird yourselves up! Take heart!"[4] It was the people's duty to be optimistic, and to fight for their people's future in the long term.

In the story, after experiencing some victories, the Chichimecs find themselves at a low point, living as the dependents of a more powerful ethnic state whose people had been in the region far longer than they. They are frequently demeaned and cannot worship their own gods properly. But they have no weapons, no way of fighting back. Then Tezcatlipoca speaks to them, and helps them devise a clever plan. They are to offer to take responsibility for organizing the festivities of an upcoming holiday. There would be ceremonial dancing—dancing that required weapons. Their leader goes to speak to the overlords, asking permission for his people to collect broken, cast-off weapons for use in the performance. He returns having secured the permission and addresses the community with tears in his eyes. "O my children, o Tolteca, go to it with a will!" he cries.

> Then they dispersed and went to do the borrowing, saying to the town's residents, "Please lend us your old weapons, some of your old shields and war clubs—not your good equipment—if you gave us that we would break it."
>
> "What will you do with them? What do you want them for?"
>
> "Listen, we are going to perform for the rulers. It's for when we will dance in the homes, the households, of your altepetl."
>
> "Maybe you want our good weapons?"
>
> "No, my child, just your old weapons that lie fallen where you throw out the ash water. Let's fix them up, and with them we will entertain the rulers and lords."
>
> Then the [others] said, "Fine. Here and there our old weapons, our old shields, our old clubs, are lying around. Gather them up. In fact, we don't even need our new weapons." So then the people wandered everywhere, looking in the various houses and patios. Wherever they went, there was eating and drinking going on. The residents spoke to them. They just belittled them and laughed at them. But the Chichimecs, they prepared themselves.[5]

The Tolteca Chichimeca worked late into the night, gluing, painting, and repairing, turning the battered old objects into strong and beautiful weapons. "The sufferings that the Tolteca Chichimeca endured were very great," sighed the storyteller. But they were determined to save their people's future, left without allies as they were. And in the end, they prevailed.

FROM THE SEVEN CAVES TO THE ISLAND CITY

Meanwhile, far to the north, there lived people who still knew nothing of the glories of Tollan, its tragic dissolution, or the fate of its wandering people. These were people who, the storytellers said, were still so wild that they lived in caves. But all that was about to change… The Mexica regularly settled in to listen to this tale. Judging from the number of times it was told and recorded, it was the narrative that the Mexica loved most, far more than they cared for the story of Tollan, which they tended to render in the briefest of forms or even embed within this narrative. As the Mexica people had been among the last to arrive in the central basin, it is logical that they found most compelling the tale of later arrivals.

This land to the north, said the storytellers, was called Aztlan. The word *aztatl* means "heron," and in the colonial era, some Nahuatl speakers hesitantly said that Aztlan denotes "Place of the Herons," but a grammatical analysis indicates that the name would then have to be Aztatlan. Technically, Aztlan translates as "Place of the Tools."[6] A few narrators expanded on the idea of the watery home that herons would need and said that Aztlan was an island, but most described it as being full of the thorny mesquite shrubs that grow in desert environments. In any event, the Mexica people, who lived here in a place called Chicomoztoc ("Seven Caves"), were directed by their god, Huitzilopochtli, to leave Aztlan so that they might

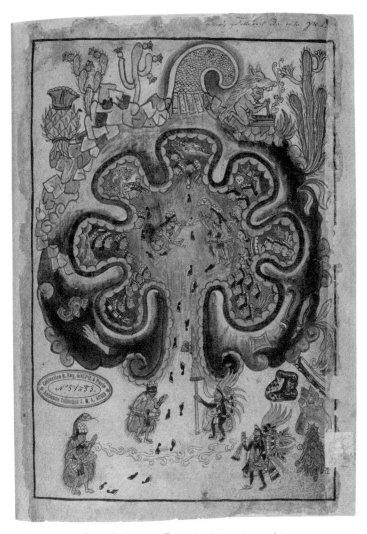

The Historia Tolteca Chichimeca offers a detailed rendering of the Seven Caves.

live life to the fullest. Some said there were four calpolli (or kin groups), but most said there were seven, one in each of the seven caves. In either case, four priests acted as "god-bearers." They were the ones who literally carried the sacred bundles understood to make Huitzilopochtli visible and recognizable to humans. Their names were usually Cuauhcoatl, Apanecatl, Tezcacohuacatl, and Chimalman. Variations on the first three names would continue to be used as titles for powerful leaders for generations. Chimalman (meaning "She Laid out Shields") was a woman, and her name would be given to important princesses far into the future. At Quinehuayan (literally, "The Place of Afterward Departing"), eight other altepetls emerged from caves and asked to join the Mexica. Which groups these were differed from version to version, but they invariably featured the groups with whom the storyteller's own generation or sub-group shared a recent history of important political ties and conflicts. Always included were the Huexotzinca, the Chalca, the Xochimilca, and the Tepaneca. The Mexica happily accepted them as fellow travelers. Thus at first it seemed as though the Mexica were destined to be the good friends of all these groups.[7]

Yet before they had gone far, everything changed. Sometimes, it seemed, sad as it was, humans could not make common cause with others and needed to look out for their own interests; indeed, this was a central tension in human life, according to the teller of the tale. The Mexica stopped to rest under a towering tree—a ceiba tree, said some, a cypress tree, said others. A huge limb broke off and fell, nearly killing them. It meant that their branch of the family was to split from the trunk. To be sure that they understood, Huitzilopochtli spoke from the upper reaches of the tree, telling them they must not go forward with their companions. At his direction, the Mexica

Where and What was Aztlan?

Many people have tried to determine exactly where the homeland called Aztlan was, but such a task is futile, as Uto-Aztecan peoples migrated from various places over multiple centuries. All the Nahuas of central Mexico, not just the Mexica—even those who did not use the place name "Aztlan"—described their ancient homeland similarly. They all believed that in that northern land there were seven caves (Chicomoztoc) from which their people had emerged. Even if we focus on the Mexica alone, we must confront the fact that they paused repeatedly in their long migration. Their ancestors, like everyone else's, had come across the Bering Strait many generations earlier and spent millennia moving southward. Still, it seems clear from linguistic evidence that there was a long period of residence in what is today the Southwestern United States, so it seems relatively safe to assume that the storied place of origin refers to that area.

A few of the sources assume that the place of origin was an island—probably because they thought the word for "heron," *aztatl*, was embedded in "Aztlan," and herons, of course, rely on their ability to fish in wetlands. Most of the sources, however, remember the northern homeland as a desert, as indeed it was. Lovely birds figured prominently in references to Aztlan. They represented warriors who had bravely died for their people in ancient times (as well as more recent times) and gone on to an afterlife reserved for them.

Pictorial sources show the people migrating southward from Aztlan and the Seven Caves, their treks memorialized by images of footprints and glyphs representing notable places where they stopped and spent time. One text, the Codex Aubin, calls these people on the move the "Azteca," meaning "people of Aztlan." In the eighteenth century, scholars saw this and seized upon the word as a term for the sixteenth-century power that dominated central Mexico. But by that time, as the Codex Aubin itself said, the people called themselves the Mexica. "Aztec" had only ever been a word from a story about a mythical place called Aztlan.

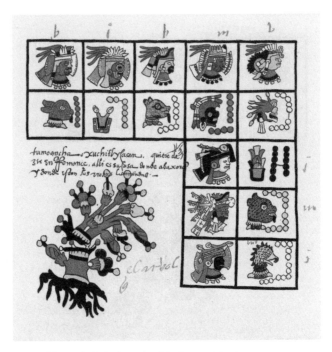

The symbolic broken tree of the Aztec origin story appears
in the Codex Telleriano-Remensis.

departed on their own, and for many pages, the tale describes them as migrating through the lands of central Mexico, staying here for four years, or there for twenty, but always moving on again, always relatively friendless. Still, in their wanderings, they gained many gifts, among them honey, pulque, arrows and the *atlatl*, their deadly spear-thrower. And their experiences toughened them up, teaching them to count on no one but themselves.

Eventually the Mexica came to Chapultepec ("Grasshopper Hill"), the very spot that is now a major tourist attraction in Mexico City.

There they lived happily for twenty years. But their chief, Huitzilihuitl ("Hummingbird Feather"), put on airs, grabbed women from other altepetls and generally offended the people who surrounded them, most notably, the Culhuaque of Culhuacan ("The Place of People who had Ancestors"). So the Culhuaque gathered their allies together and came to destroy them. All the Mexicas' leading nobles were taken captive and divvied up among the altepetls who had come to make war. Huitzilihuitl and his daughter were taken to Culhuacan, the most important town of the Culhuaque people. "They went naked. They no longer had anything on. In Culhuacan there was a king whose name was Coxcox. Huitzilihuitl really pitied his daughter, who didn't even have one little thing on. He said to the king, 'O lord, allow my daughter a little something.' But the other man said, 'No, I do not want that. She will stay as she is.'"[8]

The Codex Aubin shows the arrival of the Mexica at Chapultepec ("Grasshopper Hill").

The Codex Aubin tells the classic tale, showing when the beleaguered
Mexica people were taken prisoner.

The girl, whose name was usually given as Chimalxochitl ("Shield
Flower"), was very proud and very fierce. The Mexica would be proud
of her for many generations to come. She sat as if disdainful. Days went
by, while the Culhuaque searched the nearby swamplands for Mexica
who had fled the battle. There in the wetlands the survivors were
enduring great trials. "The common people are suffering, are enduring
hardship," said one of their leaders. "Let us perhaps go to light fires,
or sweep [as servants]. Let us enter under the rule of the lords [of
Culhuacan]." And so they sent a delegation. Arrangements for peace
were made, and the people began to trickle into Culhuacan, where
they saw Chimalxochitl in her prison. Till now, she had remained
impassive, but at the sight of her people, she began to shout. "Why do
we not die?!" she demanded. "Let the lords listen! Let us ask for the
chalk and the feathers!" Everyone knew that people who were to be

sacrificed were given holy chalk marks and decorated with feathers, so her meaning was clear. Her father agreed with her, and the two were given what they demanded. They decorated themselves—since no one else seemed to have the courage for it—and then they died. "When they first set fire to the honored woman, she exclaimed as she wept, she said to those below, 'O people of Culhuacan, I go to where the divine lives. My hair and my nails will all become warriors!'" In speaking of her hair and her fingernails, which do not rot immediately when a person dies, she used a common metaphor, meaning that what was left of her—what remained of her people—would grow to be great. After she died, the Culhuaque washed away her blood, but they could not wash away the words she had uttered.[9]

After the sacrifice of the chief and his daughter, King Coxcox of Culhuacan let the ordinary Mexica people go and settle at Tizaapan

Eventually, an eagle lands on a cactus as the Mexica build their temple.

("Chalky Place by the Water"), at the edge of the great lake that filled the middle of the central basin of Mexico. He thought that they would be miserable in a muddy region infested by snakes. However, the Mexica, who had often hidden out there, were a step ahead of him. One narrator joked, "The Mexica were overjoyed when they saw the snakes. They cooked them all; they roasted them up and ate them."[10] They thought that there in that land which no one else wanted they would at last be able to live in peace. But before they knew it, Coxcox began to place impossible demands on them, designed both to show them up and to give him the right to punish them. First he demanded that they find a way to move a field full of plants, in which would be found a crane and a snake. With the help of Huitzilopochtli, they managed it, cutting sod and bringing the field a little at a time. "Who *are* these Mexica?" asked the Culhuaque. Next Coxcox demanded that they bring him a deer without any puncture wounds or any broken bones. This they managed to do almost by accident, driving their quarry into a place so muddy that he got stuck. Again the Culhuaque were impressed and even frightened. "Who *are* these Mexica?!" they asked themselves.[11]

Now Coxcox came up with what he thought would be a permanent answer to the question of what to do with these neighbors who made him nervous. He told them that they could go forage for needed supplies in the lands of the Xochimilca, and then sent word to the Xochimilca that they should ambush the Mexica. But the Mexica had been prepared for a trap: They fought so hard that every one of them killed at least two of their enemies. Determined to show the Culhuaque not to mess with them, they cut off the noses of every single one of their victims and placed them in bags. (Though it would have been easier to cut the ears, they decided not

THE BEGINNINGS OF HUMAN SOCIETY

Chinampas

Any cultivated field (*milli*, or in some contexts *milpa*) had sacred
qualities and could symbolize the earth as a whole. Even more special
was a *chinampa* (from *chinamitl*, a fence made of plants, or that
which could be enclosed in such a fence). Because the Aztecs did
not have much arable land in their lacustrine environment, they
learned to build little fields in shallow water. They put down stakes
in the lake, and wove reeds between them, creating an enclosure,
which they then filled with earth, building it up carefully in layers.
Sometimes they stabilized the structure by planting willows at
the corners. In these damp, nutrient-rich gardens, crops grew
abundantly. Indeed, they still do in the area near Xochimilco
("Flowering Fields"), south of Mexico City. Most of the great lake
was drained long ago, during the colonial era, so such "floating
gardens" have become rare. But recently this agricultural technique
has been making a comeback.

Detail of a modern painting of *chinampas* by Mexican artist José Muro Pico.

to, the narrator said a tad snarkily, lest anyone accuse them of trying to double count. What they had done was quite ferocious enough!)

At last Coxcox decided to relent: he gave the Mexica permission to bury a sacred bundle and build a temple, and then to hold a ceremony in which they would tie together and record fifty-two years for the first time. He came to see the celebration. (Some said he was invited, so the Mexica could show off for him; others said he came in secret to observe because he was so concerned. "I would like to see what the Mexica are up to!"[12]) The Mexica had saved two (or was it four?) Xochimilca prisoners from those who tried to ambush them, and these they now sacrificed, burning them on the altar. Two divine beings became visible to those who were present. (One narrator in the sixteenth century, himself probably a Christian, hastened to explain, "It was not truly them, but that is indeed how they saw it."[13] Then he went right on with his story without further interruption.) One was called Xiuhcoatl ("Turquoise Snake") or Xiuhchimalliquetzalpanitl ("Turquoise Shield Quetzal Banner"), either probably a poetic name for the being the Spaniards heard called Xiuhteuctli ("Turquoise Lord"), an ancient spirit of the hottest fire. "While the sacrifice was being made, the Mexica and Coxcox heard a shriek from the sky. At that an eagle came down, alighting on the peak of the temple's thatch house. What he placed there was something like a nest, upon which he stood."[14]

These were clear signs that the Mexica were meant to be there, but their troubles were not yet over. They had to continue to fight for their ground, and indeed, they had to move on once again before their wanderings were finished. While some of the Mexica had been living in the swamps after the battle with the Culhuaque, one of their noblewomen had borne a child, named Axolotl (a kind of edible salamander), or, some said, Axolohua (possessor of such salamanders). When he was grown, he wandered one day in the swamps with some companions, and there he sank in the water. He visited the land of Tlaloc, and, miraculously, returned to his people. He told them: "I saw Tlaloc, and he spoke to me and said, 'My child Huitzilopochtli has exhausted himself coming here [meaning: is welcome here]. His home will be here, he will be valued [cared for], so that we may live together on earth.'"[15] There could be no further arguing. The Mexica would not move again, come what may. It was settled. The leader of each calpolli (kin group) made a moving speech in order to confirm the social contract. Here, on an island in the middle of the great lake, was where Tenochtitlan would be. The Mexica people had struggled and survived. They had earned their land and home, as they put it.

OTHER PERSPECTIVES ON THE LONG MIGRATION

It was not only the Mexica who had made their way from the north country to the central basin of Mexico. All the many groups of Nahuatl speakers had; the Mexica were just among the last to arrive. So all the Nahuas told similar stories about their ancestors making their way down from caves where they once lived to join the agriculturalists of the flowered lands in the south. But their perspectives on the great drama varied considerably. At root, there was a certain commonality: They were all preoccupied with the question of the making and breaking of alliances, and hence of the potential for violence. Beyond that, however, their concerns were quite different. Those who had been in central Mexico longest identified more fully as agriculturalists, and therefore were less invested in praising fast-moving nomadic warriors above all others. But people who had arrived not long before the Mexica tended to focus instead either on having remained unbeaten by them, or else on having had the good sense to befriend them early on in their career and remain steadfastly loyal.

In Cuauhtinchan, in the valley to the east of the central valley, the storytellers said that after the people had survived the break-up of Tollan and the ensuing adventures (including the successful attack on their enemies using the ruse of hosting a great dance celebration), the leaders Icxicohuatl ("Footed Snake") and Quetzaltehueyac ("Long Quetzal Feather") had to travel north to the land of Chicomoztoc, where the rest of the Chichimeca were still living. They needed them to fight on their side in a great war. Outside the mountain sheltering the Seven Caves, they could hear a buzzing like that of bees and wasps. Quetzaltehueyac broke open the mountain with his staff, and when he drew it out a bee was clinging to it. Out popped Cohuatzin ("Honored Snake"), who was a speaker of Nahuatl, an interpreter. He looked at the newcomers. "Who are you? Where did you come from? What are you looking for?" he wanted to know. They answered that they had come looking for the Chichimeca, as the one "who was two, who was three" had great need of them. So Cohuatzin went back into the mountain, where the Chichimecs were waiting to hear what he had to say: "'Who are they?' And Cohuatzin answered: 'Listen, this is what they say: They came to take you. The one who is two, who is three, needs you and seeks you.'" Cohuatzin came back out of the cave and said to Quetzaltehueyac that the Chichimecs' response was that "the one who was two, who was three" was not *their* creator! Quetzaltehueyac found he had to speak more bluntly. He needed to tell them that they were to be given gifts far greater than those they had had before: He was going to make sedentary farmers out of them. He put it thus: "I am the one who has come to make you leave your life in caves and hills." Cohuatzin went back down into the cave and repeated that message. The Chichimeca responded that if that were so, Quetzaltehueyac must give them a name, some special words. Cohuatzin went back out and repeated the message. In response, Quetzaltehueyac and Icxicohuatl sang a beautiful song in Nahuatl. Cohuatzin went back down inside and repeated it.[16]

And then the Chichimec people of Cuauhtinchan began to realize the power of what was being offered. Cohuatzin stepped forward and said, "Am I alone sought and needed for the divine water and fire [that is, for war]?" Cohuatzin went back out and spoke to Quetzaltehueyac and Icxicohuatl, saying, on behalf of the Cuauhtinchan Chichimeca, "Will I alone meet [or see] the fields, the divine earth?" But they answered that on the contrary, all who surrounded him on left and right, all the many groups, should leave the "cave and hilltop life.… All would meet [see] the fields and divine earth, all would be the possessors of the flowering plants." This statement had a powerful effect, perhaps especially on the women, who had long been the ones in charge of all plant-gathering. "There was an exodus of all the Chichimec men and Chichimec women." They went proudly, singing "To war! To war!" knowing well that that was why they were needed, but glad of the gifts of agriculture they were to receive in recompense. Soon, they were indeed given the gift of corn, as well as the Nahuatl language. The Cuauhtinchan people who told the story were evidently very proud of both sides of their heritage, the nomadic and the agricultural.

Quite different was the situation of the people of Tlaxcala, who had arrived around the same time as the Mexica. With a large population of their own, they had made a career of remaining determinedly independent of the famous altepetl on the rise. (Indeed, they were still the Mexicas' most powerful enemies when the Spaniards arrived, and they ended up allying with Hernando Cortés.) In their story of the passage from the northland to their new home in the valley just to the east of the central basin, the Tlaxcalteca envisioned themselves not as the Mexica did (hard-pressed, but stubborn), but rather, as almost glamorous in their ferocity. When they left Chicomoztoc, they were guided by a leader named Ce Tecpatl, literally "One Flint Knife," a calendrical day sign referencing the tool used to cut victims open for sacrifice. As the Tlaxcalteca wended their way south, they hunted and made war:

> They lived carrying their bows and arrows. It is said
> that they had sting arrows, fire arrows, and arrows that
> followed people. It is even said that their arrows could
> seek things out. When they would go hunting, their

A prince of Tlaxcala from an early post-conquest drawing.

arrow could go anywhere. If it was going along hunting
something up above, they would see the arrow coming
back with an eagle. If their arrow saw nothing above, it
came back down to fall upon something, maybe a puma
or ocelot, snake or deer, rabbit or quail. They went along
to see what their arrow had brought down![17]

They were fierce in defense of their sovereignty, but also good at
making friends, so as to be able to deal with their enemies (especially
the Mexica) with brutal effectiveness. It was exhausting. By the time
they arrived at the mountain they called Tlaxcalticpac ("Atop the
Ridge of the Tortilla") the nine god-bearers who carried their sacred
bundles and holy fire starters were quite ready to settle down.

According to another set of stories, the people of Cuauhtitlan were
longtime neighbors and friends of the Mexica, living to the north of
the great lake in the central basin. (Their chiefly lines were in fact
related.) They, too, told of the Chichimecs exiting Chicomoztoc and
embarking on a long peregrination. "They were hunters on the move.
They had no houses, no lands, and no soft clothes or cloaks. They
just wore hides and long moss. And their children were raised up
in mesh bags and pack baskets."[18] They remembered Tezcatlipoca
(under the name of Yaotl, or "War") warning them not to become
arrogant. If they did, he would mock them with unexpected events,
as he had mocked a certain king of Toltec Mountain. Snorted Yaotl:
"[That king] had two daughters ... whom he kept in a jeweled cage.
I got them pregnant with twins!"[19] The narrator tracked the forging
of alliances between different Chichimec groups and their breaking
asunder; he described where each sub-group eventually settled in
a long and complex text. Eventually he arrived at the point in the

story where the Mexica were at Chapultepec and alienated their neighbors, bringing on the devastating attack led by the Culhuaque. The people of Cuauhtitlan were invited to join in the despoiling of the Mexica. "But the chief would not consent; he did not want that. Right away he sent messengers to assure the Mexica that the people of Cuauhtitlan would not be their enemies."[20] In fact, the messenger carried gifts as well—quail, turkey eggs, and little snakes, which the Mexica were known to love.

That loyal Cuauhtitlan chief, named Quinantzin, heard about the disaster the Mexica people suffered, and the fact that the king and his daughter, Chimalxochitl, had been taken to Culhuacan as prisoners. At this point, the Cuauhtitlan people's version of the story suddenly took a dramatic turn that would have been a surprise to any Mexica listeners, since they remembered the two prisoners as having been dramatically sacrificed. "The ruler Quinantzin gave the order [to his people] to save them." Despite the difficulties of such a feat, they managed it, and brought Chimalxochitl back to Quinantzin. "When the ruler saw her, he loved her. He was about to go to her and lie with her." But the young woman was not interested: "She did not consent. She just said, 'Not yet, my lord, for I am fasting. That which you desire may be done later, for I am a sweeper [a woman in religious service]. The vow I make is for just two more years; it will be finished in two more years, my lord. Please give the order to have the people prepare for me a little altar of beaten earth, so that I can make offerings to my god, place my sacred pot, and fast.'" Quinantzin honored the valiant Mexica woman's request; then, two years later, they were married. They had two children. The father named the first one, but Chimalxochitl did not like the name he chose. She herself named the second, calling him Tezcatl Teuctli

("Mirror Lord") in honor of her own god, Tezcatlipoca. "And it was he who became [the next] ruler of Cuauhtitlan," added the narrator, demonstrating the woman's power.[21]

Now the royal houses of the Mexica and the Cuauhtitlan people were even more tightly connected. And the Cuauhtitlan storyteller's sympathy for the Mexica increased in direct proportion. He remembered them being treated abominably by the Culhuaque, who at one point even deceptively called away the Mexica men so the Tepaneca could enter the village and have their way with the women. "They fell upon the women over at Chapultepec. They really finished them off, then robbed them. And when they dashed them to the ground, then they raped them gratuitously. The Mexica were already losing, over where they were engaged in combat."[22] Could the Mexica be blamed, asked their friends, if they later became a tad too violent? Indeed, they could not.

Nevertheless, perhaps in an effort to hedge their bets, the Cuauhtitlan royal family maintained ties with their counterparts in Culhuacan as well. There was another romantic marriage to recount:

It happened one time that the ruler of Cuauhtitlan,
Huactli [the name of a bird], went hunting, and he ended
up meeting a young woman at the place called Tepolco.
He did not know whether this young woman was a
noblewoman. At length he asked her. He said, "Who
are you? Whose daughter are you? Where do you come
from?" She answered him, saying, "Lord, my home is
in Culhuacan, and my father is the king, Coxcox." "And
what does he call you? What is your name?" "My name
is Iztolpanxochitl [the name of a lovely flower]." When

Huactli heard this, he took her home with him and made her his wife. And he had children with her.[23]

One of those children, Iztactototl ("White Turkey"), grew up and went to war, and in the emotion of that moment, decided he wished to see his grandfather, King Coxcox of Culhuacan. He went to visit him, and the old man was pleased. He said, "I am an old man, already dying. Here in Culhuacan it is you who will be ruler. You will be ruler of the Culhuaque." But Iztactototl, who had some powers as if he were an oracle, just laughed and said, "Whose ruler would I be? For the Culhuacan altepetl is not to endure. It is to crumble and be dispersed."[24] King Coxcox was enraged and demanded to know just exactly how that was to happen! But of course, the boy proved to be right. Culhuacan slipped into the shadows as the star of the Mexica rose. The Mexica themselves believed that Chimalxochitl had in effect foretold it when she died ("My hair and my nails will all become warriors!"). In the memory of the Cuauhtitlan people, it was a little prince of theirs who had seen clearly what was to happen. They were content to have understood and befriended power.

SMOKE RISING

Though each altepetl had its own perspective on the past, everyone agreed that the Mexica city of Tenochtitlan eventually grew to be the most impressive place their world had ever seen. Years later, one of the foot soldiers who accompanied Hernando Cortés was stunned by his first view of the Aztecs' great city. The Spaniards had climbed over the ring of mountains that surrounded the central valley of Mexico

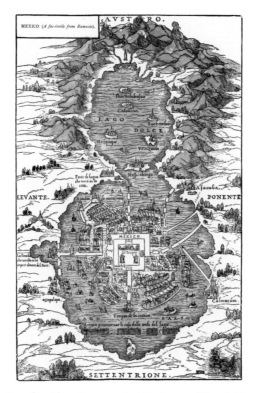

From the 16th century onward, stylized maps of Tenochtitlan
were published in numerous European books.

and were approaching the giant lake at the center of the basin. Smaller
towns with their chinampas dotted its banks, and on an island in the
center rose the towering temples and substantial palaces of a great
urban power. "When we saw all those villages built in the water …
and the straight and level causeway leading to the City of Mexico,
we were astounded. These great pyramids and buildings rising from
the water, all made of stone, seemed like an enchanted vision."[25]

Tenochtitlan

From its humble origins, Tenochtitlan grew into a monumental capital. In the very center of the city, on a great plaza, builders gradually turned what had originally been a simple temple dedicated to Huitzilopochtli into a huge, imposing pyramid for him. Next to it they constructed a twin temple dedicated to Tlaloc. They painted the buildings with lime, which glistened white in the sunlight, and decorated the two towers with bright paint and colorful banners that whipped in the wind. The *tlatoani*'s huge U-shaped compound centered around a courtyard where performers came to sing, dance, and tell stories. The haunting music of conch shells drew the people; the throbbing of the drums might continue late into the night on festive occasions. Inside, the high chief and his officials maintained a library of pictographic scrolls, used to record tribute owed, tribute paid, and other matters. In another sector, a zoological garden displayed the exotic birds and animals collected from the realms conquered by the Mexica. In an aviary, palace employees bred tropical birds so that their neon feathers could be used to weave beautiful cloaks and shield covers.

In the neighborhoods round about lived more ordinary people. The roofs of their one- and two-storied houses were lined with gardens visible from the street, and songbirds were everywhere. Everyone worked hard. Boys mostly learned the artisan trades of their fathers, but when they were young adolescents, they went away to school so that they could become warriors—or priests, if that was their fate. Girls worked with their mothers, perfecting their skills in spinning, weaving, sewing, and embroidering; those destined to become priestesses also went to school.

But that moment was two hundred years in the future. Tenochtitlan's origins were both humble and beautiful. The people had sought "the altepetl of Mexico Tenochtitlan, the place of renown, the sign, the site of the rock tuna cactus, in the middle of the water;

On the northern shore of the island lay a great market, easily reachable by canoes coming from all the villages lining the shores of the extensive lake. There people could find all manner of food, including caged turkeys and other birds. They could buy furs and hides and cloth, precious feathers and stones, or the clothes and jewelry that were made of them. They could find ceramic ware, copper needles, obsidian blades and mirrors, sandals, rubber balls, and maguey paper. There were even barbers with stands and food-sellers serving lunch.

Like all great powers, the world of the Mexica was partly based on the labor of others. Some of the goods being sold in the market had been delivered as tribute payments by conquered *altepetls*. And there were slaves for sale, too, mostly young women and children who had been taken in war. A few of them would face sacrifice in ritual ceremonies; we can barely imagine the agonies they experienced as they waited to learn their fate. Most of the enslaved, however, would become domestic servants in the wealthy houses that surrounded them. At least they could tell themselves that their fate was theirs alone; their children would be free: They would be raised as citizens of this most extraordinary city.

Today only remnants of the place that once held visitors spellbound are visible in the archaeological site of the Templo Mayor (great temple) on the plaza now called the Zócolo. After the arrival of the Spaniards, a cathedral was built almost on top of the old temple, and the rest of the city was gradually transformed until it became the Mexico City we know today.

the place where the eagle rests, where he screeches, where he stretches and eats; where the serpent hisses, where the fish fly, where the blue and yellow waters mingle."[26] The Mexica planted their town on the island very purposely and self-consciously, so unlike the ancient

European cities that the Spaniards were accustomed to seeing; it had not grown in a sprawling, unplanned way, with winding streets and narrow alleys, but had been designed and built with an eye to what we might today call city planning. The result was that straight, clean-swept roads led from the lakeshore over carefully engineered causeways and on into the heart of the orderly island city.

The Mexica began by building their first small temple, pounding down the earth and sweeping it relentlessly to make a platform for a small pyramid. Later, they would build much larger ones, but they weren't ready for that just yet. In the evening, they went fishing in the lake and then put their catch to broil. The delicious-smelling smoke rose in the air. As such smoke so often did in Nahuatl narratives, it drew their enemies.[27] But those who came to fight them could not vanquish the newcomers, who were determined to do whatever it took so that they could stay in this place.

Human nature being what it is, the Mexica had generations of struggle to face—arguments within the group, and arguments with their neighbors. But the people were determined to meet the challenge—to find a way to survive and succeed without becoming arrogant. It was a tall order. They prayed to Tezcatlipoca, "If perhaps one should become arrogant, if perhaps one should become presumptuous, if perhaps one should become offensive, should keep for oneself your property, your possessions, if one should become perverse or heedless, you will give it all to the truly tearful, the sorrowful, the sighing one, the person worthy of compassion."[28] Such was their ancient, oft-repeated prayer. Yet there were times when it would prove difficult to remember.

4

LEGENDS OF HISTORY

At night, in [King] Huitzilihuitl's sleep, the god Yohualli ["Night"] spoke to him. He said, "We shall go among them in Cuernavaca. We shall go to the home of Lord Ozomatzin ['He Got Angry'], and we shall take his daughter named Miyahuaxihuitl ['Corn Tassel Gem']." And when Huitzilihuitl awoke, he sent emissaries to Cuernavaca to ask for Miyahuaxihuitl as a wife. Lord Ozomatzin heard the words by which the Mexica asked for his daughter. But he just went up to the marriage-makers and he said, "What is Huitzilihuitl saying?! What will he give my daughter there in the middle of the water? Perhaps he will clothe her with marsh plants and marsh plant thread, as he clothes himself with breechclouts of marsh plant thread?! And what will he give her to eat? … Go tell your ruler Huitzilihuitl, tell him definitely: you are not to come here again."[1]

One day, a full generation after the Spanish conquest, an Indigenous man from Cuauhtitlan sighed in vexation: He had two old histories laid out before him and did not know what to do about an obvious contradiction in them. He decided to follow his people's ancient tradition and give both accounts, rather than taking on the role of omnipotent narrator and choosing between them. However, as a boy, this man had been educated by the Franciscans, and his training with them had led him to believe that such decisions were supposed to be his to make as the writer. So after he copied out the second version of events, he added, still in Nahuatl, "This genealogical statement cannot be true. The truth of how things were arranged has already been stated."[2]

Historians ever since have often suffered in much the same way, worrying about discrepancies in the old historical tales left to us by the Aztecs. But there is no need for such preoccupation. We do not need to know if a man inherited a kingship when he was seven years old or nine years old, or if his wife was a young aunt or a cousin. What we need to know, in order to understand that man's situation, is that he inherited the kingship very young (and why this was so), and that he married a close relative (and why). Nahuatl-language legendary histories deftly lead their hearers (or readers) to the heart of political situations that once were very real. Especially when they are speaking of events within about a hundred years before the conquest, they are illuminating of the essential elements of those historical situations, if not always of the exact details.

THE POLITICAL DRAMA OF POLYGAMY

Aztec legendary histories often seem, at the very beginning, as though they are going to be all about war. One group enters the territory of another group. They hunt and cook. The smoke rises, alerting those who have long lived in the area of the presence of potential enemies. Said one Chichimec chief: "Who are these people making smoke at the edge of the woods? O fathers [beloved people], go shoot them with arrows or kill them, for they have fallen into our hands

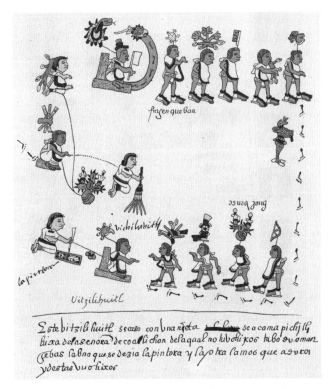

This page of the Codex Telleriano-Remensis conveys the political complexities arising from the fact that a king (in this case, Huitzilihuitl) always had multiple wives.

and are already our prisoners!"[3] Yet ultimately this very narrative, like so many others, becomes a story not of battles, but rather, of marriages. This was so for a good reason: almost all Aztec political complexities were connected to the phenomenon of polygamy. In noblemen's households there lived a range of women by whom they had children—from a leading or primary wife to secondary wives to concubines and slaves—and there were always political ramifications.

This assertion of the political dimension of marriages should not be understood as an indication that wars were easily prevented simply by arranging a marriage between two royals of two different city-states, or that wars occurred when such marriages failed to happen. That is not a realistic way to think about history. By way of comparison, one might consider Queen Victoria's rather ineffective policy of marrying her children all across Europe, which did nothing to prevent the First World War. The experienced Nahuas were not so naïve as to imagine that marriages would necessarily cement peace. Their histories are full of weddings, and sometimes the alliances proved effective—but sometimes they merely led to strain and even death for foreign spouses when their peoples returned to a state of war.[4] No, the Nahuas weren't necessarily seeking peace. Rather, they used marriage as a tool to structure political relationships between altepetls. A powerful city-state could demand that a less powerful city-state provide their chief with a lesser wife who, it was understood, would not inherit his kingdom, but rather, would symbolize her people's subservience (though an energetic young woman might perhaps guarantee her people certain advantages in trade and other arenas). Far worse, a powerful chief could demand that a vanquished city-state provide him a wife whose child would be raised in Tenochtitlan and develop loyalties there, but then would return to his mother's home town to rule.

Yet such arrangements, whether initially welcome or unwelcome, were not immutable, which made for a socially and politically complex world. A primary wife could lose her status if her altepetl of origin lost its paramountcy, or a lowborn concubine could gain significant power if she became a favorite. City-states could—and did—end up fighting wars to change the power relations encoded in royal marriages. Likewise, the members of large royal families who were divided into many sub-groups due to a king's having had many wives could find themselves at odds with each other. In fact, most wars between city-states were in effect also civil wars, as bands of brothers by different mothers fought about what the nature of the hierarchy between them should be. The less powerful ones could invite allies from another altepetl to side with them in a crisis, so that what was really an internal power struggle appeared on the surface to be an invasion by outsiders. In telling stories about such wars, relationships and marriages were always central elements.

Before Tenochtitlan rose to power, the altepetl of Azcapotzalco, we recall, was dominant in the central valley, and in the stories told by other altepetls, their kings regularly abused the complex marriage system to try to gain their political ends. Their old king, Tezozomoc, tried to insist, for instance, that one of his sons by a lesser wife from Cuauhtitlan be welcomed back to his mother's home as their king. "This Tezozomoc, this ruler of Azcapotzalco, desired in his heart to make one of his children the ruler of Cuauhtitlan." But the people of Cuauhtitlan did not feel that Azcapotzalco had enough power over them to justify his making this demand. "The Chichimec nobles would not consent. Tezozomoc got really frustrated that his son was not received as ruler of Cuauhtitlan—for indeed, he had killed their late ruler!"[5]

When this old king Tezozomoc died, he left various sons by different women ruling in various city-states. One of these, named Maxtla ("Breechclout" or "Loincloth"), to whom he had bequeathed a lesser chiefdom, wanted what his half-brother by another mother had received—the rulership of the great city of Azcapotzalco. So he attacked his half-brother and that brother's supporters and took over

A Marriage Ceremony

Aztec noblemen were wealthy enough to be able to support multiple wives. The vast majority of men, however, had only one wife, one partner for life. When a boy wished to marry, his elders had a meeting and decided which young woman "to ask for." The women—or their chosen matchmakers—went to the young lady's household, bringing gifts. If it seemed to go well, then each day for several days, early in the morning, they returned to make their case. Once the matter was agreed, the men in the groom's family asked the soothsayers, the *tonalpouhque* who could read the sacred calendar, to choose a good day, and the women launched the preparation of the food. "For two or three days they made tamales. They passed the whole night doing so. They slept but a little bit."[6]

At last the day came. "When it had dawned, when the groom was to marry the bride and the bride was to marry the groom, then all the invited guests entered the house." The women came bearing gifts, maguey fiber or cotten cloaks, parcels of dried corn. All the guests were given food and drink and wreaths of flowers to wear, and spent a happy day together. Old people were allowed to become quite tipsy, though young people were not.

Meanwhile, over in the bride's house, the girl was ceremonially bathed, and decorated with colored paint and precious stones and feathers. The elders in her life made speeches to her. They told her how much work was in store for a wife. "By night look to the sweeping, the tending of the fire. Arise in the deep of night. Do not embarrass us." She was to leave behind her father and her mother completely as she went to her new life. Often the daughter wept, as she thanked them for the mothering and the fathering that they had given her. When there was only a bit of daylight left, a strong older woman from among the groom's relatives came to the house and used a cloth to create a sort of sling upon her back which she used to carry the girl to her new home. "Torches were lighted, to illuminate the way to the man's place. There was a row of torch-bearers on each side, providing light. And all the women's kinsmen

Priests used books like the Codex Borgia to help them make marriage prognostications. If a ceremony was performed on a certain date, for instance, it was more likely that the groom would insist on having more than one partner. (See upper left.)

went with her, pushing toward her. It was as if the earth rumbled behind her. And as they went, all eyes were fixed upon the bride."

At the groom's home, they set the bride down next to the hearth, to the left of the groom. Their mothers gave them a gift, then tied the bride's *huipilli* (a long embroidered blouse) to the groom's cloak. The groom's mother fed each of them a tamale. They were to take four mouthfuls, emblematic of the four directions. Then the family led the two young people to a private room and locked them in. They were to have four days of alone time. After that, real life, with all its strains, would begin. But they were to try to help each other get through it all.

the city. According to one of the storytellers, the ruler of Tenochtitlan at that time, Chimalpopoca, did not approve: "It is said that he gave advice to Quetzalayatzin, whose older brother was Maxtla. He said to him, 'Little brother [meaning "friend"], why has your older brother Maxtla taken your kingdom away from you? *You* are the ruler. Your father put all of you in various offices before he died. So kill this older brother of yours, this Maxtla. He is ruling your kingdom!'"[7] Maxtla purportedly heard about this whispered conference, and had the Mexica king killed. A great war ensued, involving many altepetls. We have no way of knowing what the king of Tenochtitlan really said. What matters is that the Mexica chose to fight on the side of the ousted band of brothers in Azcapotzalco, and the storytellers, even of other altepetls, conveyed this through imaginative dialogue.

One source of power for the Mexica was in fact the adeptness with which they handled their own rivalries between brothers produced by the polygamous system in which they lived. Unlike numerous other altepetls, they managed to avoid outright civil war by constantly working to braid together the different family lines descending from different mothers. A powerful king would forego the right to have his own son or younger brother inherit after his death, and would let the pendulum of power swing back to a rival family line, provided that a daughter of his could marry the leading son of the other line, thus guaranteeing that a grandson of his would eventually rule. Or sometimes a leading contender, if he was young, would simply agree to rule later. The Aztec histories are occasionally quite explicit about the associated negotiations concerning wealth and resources.[8] But at other times they veer into smoothed-over versions that fit easily within the tradition of mini-dialogues presented to audiences on starlit evenings:

Moctezuma the Elder was the one who was supposed to
have been made ruler. It is told and related that he did not
want it. He refused, saying merely, "I will rule later. Let it
be my dear uncle Itzcoatl [who was the son of one of his
grandfather's concubines]. I wish to serve as his supporter,
putting the Mexica Tenochca in a state of readiness
concerning their food and water [their livelihood]. I will
establish their royal authority. I do not wish to be ruler.
For this reason, install me as *tlacateccatl* [the title of a
high-level counselor]. For now, let my dear uncle Itzcoatl
rule. I will depart [as a warrior] and I will provide us with
lands at the expense of those altepetls that surround us."[9]

In this world of alliances and conflicts, one's position largely
depended on who one's mother or grandmother was. We can
therefore make a case that women, through their marriages, played
a central role in politics. One might at first imagine that these marriages amounted to what we would understand as a kind of traffic
in women—that is, that the marriages represented deals made by
men and for men, that they were arrangements over which women
had absolutely no control. But we would be deluding ourselves.
The stories reveal that women in every royal palace were active
in promoting certain agendas with their menfolk, and outside
the palace, ordinary women through gossip and even loud com-
plaints could help ensure that a certain arrangement was or was
not made. In one text, the Mexica were attempting to interfere in
the affairs of the altepetl of Cuauhtinchan by placing one of their
own sons on the throne. "The honored woman named Naniotzin
["Motherhood"] spoke up. 'Is he the one who will be our ruler?!

Moctezuma II's Coronation Stone. When a new king was crowned, new building projects marked the occasion. This stone records the names of each of the Five Suns of creation: Four Ocelot, Four Wind, Four Rain, Four Water, and in the center, Nahui Olin ("Four Movement"). The boxed year sign (bottom center) is Eleven Reed, when Moctezuma became king. At the top, a day sign appears (One Crocodile), almost certainly the date of the coronation.

Is he not an Ayapaneca [that is, one of his parents came from an enemy village]? It isn't possible!"[10]

The Mexica in particular saw women as valuable players in the political game in which all humans had to participate. At every stage of life (coming of age, marriage, the birth of a child) boys and young men sat through ceremonies admonishing them to take their responsibilities to the altepetl very seriously indeed—and the speeches given to young women seem to have been even longer.[11] Through their role as mothers, women were understood to be essential to their people's future; through their role as educators, they were in some ways envisioned as the keepers of the polity. And it was understood that they had to be taught or convinced to take their role seriously. No one seemed to imagine that young women were blank slates, or even easily led. Of a young woman who seemed to insist on going her

Sculptures of women with infants have been found throughout central Mexico.

own way, it was said, "Well, can she be placed in a coffer, in a reed chest?"[12] The answer, obviously, was "No." Stories portrayed such determined women as active agents in the saving of their people. Years after the death of the semi-mythical Chimalxochitl, Mexica women were still fleeing and being dispersed when their menfolk lost a war. In one story, they escaped enslavement by floating away on the lake on the shields of their dead and dying men. They first had to hide their infants and toddlers among the reeds. The next day, when their enemies had left, they came back and found as many of them as they could, of necessity swallowing the pain of losing those who had disappeared. It was their responsibility to make sure that their altepetl had a future by raising as many of the children as they could. They had found the emotional courage to do their duty.[13]

FOUR PERIODS IN MEXICA HISTORY

Aztec legendary histories help us understand four key phases of Mexica history. First, they illuminate the early years, when the city of Tenochtitlan was settled and a royal line was established. These events occurred in approximately the 1350s, close to two hundred years before the arrival of the Europeans. Second, the histories underscore the importance of a great crisis that occurred in the late 1420s and early 1430s, in which the previously mentioned Maxtla of the city-state of Azcapotzalco was overthrown, allowing the power of the Mexica to begin to grow. Third, they speak of a rising tide of Mexica power between the 1450s and the 1470s. And fourth, they focus our attention on a series of late imperial crises that occurred in the final decades before the arrival of the Spaniards, and indeed

TENOCHTITLAN'S ROYAL FAMILY

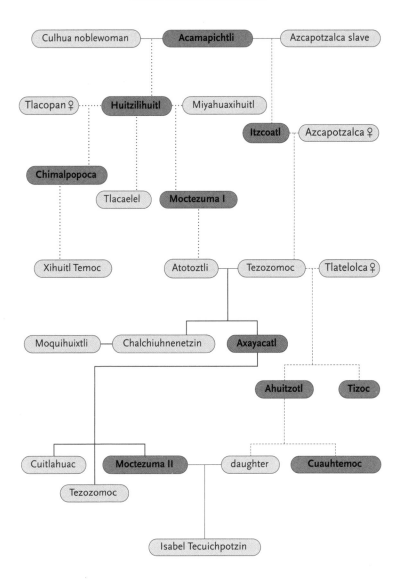

set the stage for that crisis. These stories were not all literally true in every particular, but they nevertheless conveyed the most important truths about situations that mattered to people.

THE EARLY YEARS, c. 1350

The Mexica, we must remember, were among the last of the Nahuatl-speaking migrants to travel south from the place they called Aztlan. They arrived in central Mexico in the 1200s and for many years survived as wanderers, living as dependents, first of one group, then of another. They had leaders, of course, but neither they nor their neighbors conceived of them as having a *tlatoani*, that is, a chief or king. Tlatoani means, in the most literal sense, "he who speaks regularly." A chief was a person who spoke for the group, at the will of the group. Once he was formally and ceremonially seated on "the reed mat"—the throne—it was understood that the altepetl had arrived, that it was no longer simply a collection of people who depended on some other polity to survive. For a *tlatocayotl*—a rulership or chiefly line—to be established, the altepetl had to have lands they called their own and neighbors who conceded that they were a sovereign entity.

A tlatoani was an extremely important figure, but not in the sense of being despotic or frightening. He might sometimes be both, but that was not his accepted role. His agreed-upon role was to take responsibility for his people, and to protect them at all costs. He might lead them into war, but only if he had made it his business to ascertain first that they were likely to win—never because he wished to show off, or to take gambles hoping for his own aggrandizement.

Reed mats as portrayed in the Florentine Codex, indicating the authority of kings.

It was his job to direct his people away from fighting wars they were likely to lose. He could take many wives, but only if he had accrued enough wealth to support them all, and he must never lure away another man's wife. Greed or drunkenness on the part of leaders were utterly unacceptable; indeed, an exhibition of such traits was enough to cause a people to declare their ruler unfit.[14]

When a man became chief, he prayed aloud to Tezcatlipoca, acknowledging that he probably was not worthy, was not responsible enough for the role. But he would do his best. He spoke of what he saw for himself in his dreams: "It is the load, the burden on the back, heavy, intolerable, insupportable; the large bundle, the large carrying frame." He knew it was the same one carried by others before him who had ended up "on the reed mat, the throne." The people chanted back to him, begging him to accept, for they were without a leader. "The tail, the wing [the commoners] no longer have a mother, no longer have a father." They needed a caretaker who would look out for them. Once he had accepted, they begged him not to forget his role, not to allow his power to corrupt him, not to allow himself to slip into rages or gluttony. They affectionately called him "grandson" as he would sometimes call them "fathers" in a polite reversal: "Grasp, heed, o my grandson, o precious lord: on earth all live, all go along a mountain peak. Over there is an abyss; over here is an abyss. Nowhere is it possible [to turn]. To the left, to the right is the abyss. Do not become as a wild beast: do not completely bare your teeth, your claws. Do not become completely enraged. Do not spread fear, become thorny, become spiny. Retract your teeth, your claws."[15]

Nor was it just mortal chiefs who were to do their duty by caring for less powerful beings. Even the gods were supplicated in the same terms. When the people prayed to Tlaloc for rain, they reminded him that the weakest and most blameless beings of all—the children and the animals—were suffering as much or more than erring noblemen: "All the little creatures are suffering. The troupial bird, the roseate spoonbill drag their wings. They are upended, tumbled headfirst.

Drawings in the Florentine Codex repeatedly remind us of the Mexica's love of earth's creatures.

They open and close their beaks [from thirst]. And the animals, the four-footed ones of the lord of the near, of the nigh, just wander about. They can scarcely rise; to no purpose do they lick the ground. They are crazed for water. Already there is death, all are perishing. The common folk and the animals are dying."[16] Even the prayers to the merciless Tezcatlipoca in times of hardship were in essence requests that he do his duty and spare the powerless who had done nothing to deserve their sufferings. "O master, o lord, the altepetl is like a baby, a child." And again, "May your anger abate, may your fury be placated." And finally, "May I not have aroused your feelings, may I not have walked on your anger. O lord, perform your office, do your duty!"[17]

Since the establishment of a tlatoani, a protector, was so important, it is little wonder that numerous tales were told of the Mexicas' efforts to secure the honor of having a chief. Every version was a bit different, for tellers from different altepetls each wanted their own people to have some of the credit for what had transpired. But the bottom line was that the Mexica needed to secure the cooperation of their nearest neighbors and erstwhile enemies, the people of Culhuacan. The Culhua king had a grandson whose father had been Mexica, and they asked that he be given to them as their ruler. His name was originally Itzpapalotl (after the deity), though they would later name him Acamapichtli ("Fistful of Reeds"), in honor of the place where he would rule. They further asked that he be given a Culhua bride. Their offer was a tempting one for the Culhuaque people: The visitors were promising that Tenochtitlan's royal family would be started by a man who was half Culhua, married to a full-blood Culhua woman. Their loyalty to Culhuacan would thus almost certainly remain firm. Nevertheless, the Culhua noblemen said they

The Codex Azcatitlan represents the crisis of the Tepanec Wars. In Tenochtitlan (on the left), the family of Acamapichtli ("Fistful of Reeds") rules, and the Mexica people work busily. Then (on the right) Tezozomoc of Azcapotzalco dies, and his son Maxtla ("Breechclout" or "Loincloth") takes power and builds his domain, killing the family members of Acamapichtli (far right).

needed time to consider the proposal. Eventually, they came back with this answer, giving the last word to a woman:

> The ruler Teuctlamacazqui Nauhyotl said: "It is well, Mexica. What am I to say here in Culhuacan, but that he is truly your child, your grandson? Let him go. Take him. For he is a real man [a warrior]. If he were a woman, it would not be possible for you to take her [as a ruler]. And here is

another thing: Let him take good care of the commoners, the tail and wings. And let the priest Huitzilopochtli look after things for the One who is Near, who is Nigh, for the Night, the Wind, Warfare, Tezcatlipoca. So will he [the emissary] ask my daughter, the noblewoman Atotoztli if she will let him go? For he is her child. Will he ask her?"[18]

The Mexica responded with gratitude. They were a bit surprised when they learned that the princeling did not actually live in Culhuacan, and would have to be sought in the town of Coatlichan, but they agreed to seek him there and set off. Here the various versions of the story depart from each other. A woman named Ilancueitl ("Elder Woman

Skirt") was either his aunty or the one who became his wife. She was from this altepetl or that one, depending on the preference of the teller, and whether or not he wished his own people to be related to the Mexica royal family. But all agreed that when the young man came to Tenochtitlan, the people said, "It is good! He is welcome. And what is his name?" And the answer came, "Let it be said, Acamapichtli [Fistful of Reeds]." And they built him a home in their swamp.

This was generally thought to have occurred in the year 1367 of the western calendar. Not so many years later, when the people were ruled by Acamapichtli's son Huitzilihuitl ("Hummingbird Feather," named for Chimalxochitl's father), another foundational event occurred, and it, too, involved an important marriage. First, the storytellers placed matters solidly within the realm of actual history: At this point in Tenochtitlan's development, they explained, the people badly needed access to more cotton, which did not grow well in the central basin. They initially tried long-distance trade, "but the cotton never reached the Mexica since the Mexica were very poor." The king decided to rectify the situation by offering marriage to the daughter of the lord of Cuernavaca, one of the places where cotton grew in abundance. But Lord Ozomatzin, who had great power, including abilities as a sorcerer, would have none of it. His kingdom was rich; he could secure a better marriage for his daughter. As the chapter's opening story shows, he sent Huitzilihuitl's emissaries home in no uncertain terms.

> When Huitzilihuitl heard this, he was very disappointed
> not to have been accepted. But then once again at night,
> Yohualli spoke to him in his sleep. He said, "Do not be
> troubled. I have come to tell you how you are to do things
> so that you get Miyahuaxihuitl. Make a dart and a net

with which to shoot at the home of the Lord Ozomatzin,
where his daughter is confined. And adorn the reed
shaft most marvelously. Paint it prettily. Inside it in the
center is to go a precious green stone, most precious and
shimmering. And you will stand within their boundaries;
from there you will shoot the dart. The reed in which the
precious green stone will be inserted will fall where Lord
Ozomatzin's daughter is confined. Thus we shall get her."
And so the ruler Huitzilihuitl did so.

In real life, we know from other historical annals and from archaeology, warfare ensued, a struggle in which the Mexica used violence
to extract an agreement to a political alliance to be sealed through a
marriage. But in the stories told generations later, such things were
better left unmentioned. After all, Miyahuaxihuitl's son, Moctezuma
the Elder, later became tlatoani. It wouldn't do to speak too loudly
of the state of war that had once existed between his parents' peoples.
So the storytellers conveyed what needed to be conveyed in apocry-
phal terms. The young lady was startled when the gemstone landed
at her feet: "It fell as if given from the heavens." She took it up in her
hand and marveled. "Never had she seen the like." In her curiosity,
she popped it in her mouth. Then, by accident, she swallowed it!
In ancient native tradition, she became pregnant by the precious
stone. "It happened that Moctezuma Ilhuicaminatzin ["Moctezuma
Shot from the Heavens"] was conceived." And though it may have
seemed that she had been duped, allowing the Mexica king to get
too close to her and being pulled into his political game, she in fact
had the last laugh. For it was her son and no other wife's who became
king of untold thousands.[19]

THE CRISIS OF THE TEPANEC WARS, 1420S AND 1430S

The Tepanec people had long ruled central Mexico. Their leading settlement of Azcapotzalco, we remember, had long been the dominant city-state in the valley. Tezozomoc, Azcapotzalco's ruler of many decades, had many sons by many women. At his death, it was this fact that brought down his kingdom. His greedy son, Maxtla, we have seen, refused to settle for the town he had been given, but insisted on becoming the high king of Azcapotzalco, ousting his own half-brother. This unleashed a dangerous storm for those alive at the time—but the period of flux also brought a moment of possibility for those who previously had been marginalized, including the Mexica. Moreover, it created a delightful opportunity for storytellers to speak evocatively of the veritable spy dramas that unfolded during this time.

Chimalpopoca, the Mexica tlatoani, was no friend of Maxtla's, for Chimalpopoca's family was tightly intermarried with the family of the ousted half-brother. In one story, Maxtla directly insults Chimalpopoca by raping one of his wives when they are attending Tezozomoc's funeral. When Chimalpopoca returns home, his wife tells him what happened. Chimalpopoca panics. He understands that the violation is tantamount to a declaration of war. In his terror, he sacrifices one of his own close friends to the gods, hoping for succor. His uncle Itzcoatl, Acamapichtli's son by a concubine, is revolted. He thinks to himself that if this is what things have come to, he himself should be the ruler even though he wasn't born to it. So he cleverly gets in touch with his own in-laws, who are from another Tepanec town and are supporters of Maxtla, and arranges for them to come and trick Chimalpopoca and sacrifice him in retribution for what he has done. When the news inevitably leaks that the Tepanecs have

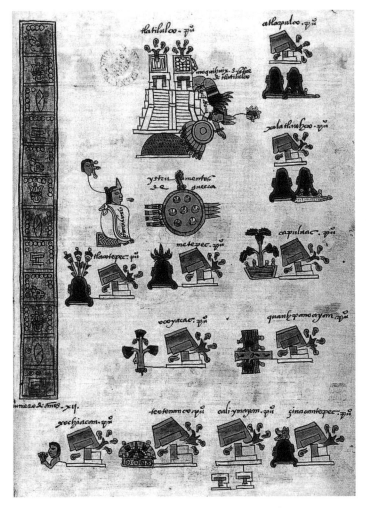

Axayacatl's reign is recorded in the Codex Mendoza, a very early post-conquest
text. In typical style, it shows all the places his warriors conquered, but it
focuses especially on the defeat of Moquihuixtli of Tlatelolco.

come into Tenochtitlan and murdered their king, the Mexica are understandably enraged and prepare for war. Itzcoatl then decides to lead them—and he himself is elected tlatoani.[20] (This story about Chimalpopoca is almost certainly not true in a literal sense: most sources agree that he was simply murdered by Maxtla's henchmen. What is important is that as the situation devolved into near chaos, Itzcoatl saw an opportunity and stepped in.)

At this point, in both the story and in life, war really broke out ("then the war spread"), as both sides sent messengers to friends and relatives in all the nearby altepetls. There were crises in Tlatelolco, Xochimilco, Texcoco, Cuauhtitlan, Chalco and other places, as all the people rushed to try to figure out which would be the winning side and get on that bandwagon. The drama—and the storied dialogue—was intense. At one point the young prince Moctezuma (who would later become tlatoani) was in Chalco with some companions rustling up support, but the tide of the discussion turned against him and he was imprisoned and slated for punitive sacrifice in the morning. But through a dream, Yohualli spoke to the local tlatoani and said—beginning humorously—"Cuateotl, are you asleep?" He answered (possibly with a sigh), "No, lord." And a very serious answer came: "Listen, they have gathered everyone together so that the Mexica [visitors] may burn at dawn, but the time has come to let them go.... The Mexica Tenochca will be [the power of the future], not the Tepaneca or the Chalca." The king went to tell the guards to let the captives go, "for the time will come when the Mexica will be our mother, will be our father." The prisoners were at first incredulous, insisting that they were brave enough to die, but then they ran. It was touch-and-go. They ultimately had to kill a recalcitrant fisherman in order to take his canoe and flee over the water.[21]

Another version likewise recalls the dialogue that "someday the Mexica Tenochca will be our mother and our father"—though it is not a god, but rather, some friendly people from Huexotzinco who say the words—and then gives a softer, more poetic cast to the predawn flight of Moctezuma and his companions. Indeed, it could be the denouement of a modern movie:

> They came to the edge of the forest and looked out
> [with concern], as if sorcerers lived in the light seeking
> them wherever they went. When they heard sandals
> crackle [behind them] they fled, as the Chalca sought
> the great Mexica lords. And they came to rest in Texcoco....
> It was dawn. The birds were already calling out. The lord
> Moctezuma said to a young man, "I am parched." Then
> the young man went to take up water with a tuna cactus,
> from which Moctezuma Shot-from-the-Sky drank. They
> spent another day where they had hidden themselves in
> Tetzitzillacatitlan, and again they slept there. And when
> it was daybreak and the birds were chattering, they fled
> as the dawn broke over them. Then they called to one
> of the fishermen, who lived by the water with a boat.
> They called to him in his Acolhua dialect; they said,
> "Bring your boat here." And the fisherman, who heard
> them, thought perhaps they were his fishermen-friends
> who called, so right away he went to bring the boat
> to the shore. Afterwards, those ... who were looking for
> the great Mexica lords beat at the fisherman with sticks
> and threw him into the water. Later he joined with those
> who were coming over the water chasing the Mexica.[22]

Stories of this time that did not emerge from Tenochtitlan but rather from other city-states cast things from a different angle, but all seemed to agree that the Tepaneca had been arrogant, and had driven away their friends, leaving them vulnerable when Itzcoatl and his followers began to seek allies. In Cuauhtitlan, for instance, they writhed under a tlatoani that Maxtla and his peers had foisted on them, so they secretly installed a ruler of their own choosing. "The only ones who knew of this were [their friends] the Mexica Tenochca." And later the storyteller spoke even more bluntly: "The Tepaneca had caused much suffering." He listed the princes they had killed and was not surprised that so many had chosen to side with the Mexica when the cataclysm came.

Perhaps the most famous drama of this time was the story that came out of Texcoco. The young prince Nezahualcoyotl ("Hungry Coyote") had seen his own father murdered by the Tepaneca because he was refusing to declare a son by one of their women his heir. Nezahualcoyotl's name is emblematic of the fact that he was born into a time when neither his altepetl of Texcoco nor his lineage within that altepetl was particularly powerful: His mother was a Mexica noblewoman. Some said Nezahualcoyotl was watching from a cave when his father was killed, and some said he was watching from a tree, but in either case, the boy fled east, and lived at the mercy of various friends and relatives among the people of Huexotzinco and Tlaxcala. When the Mexica decided to rise against Maxtla of Azcapotzalco, Nezahualcoyotl, by then a grown man, was the first ally that they sought out, and he joined them eagerly. He went to visit his old connections in the region, and promised them release from paying tribute to the Tepaneca if they would help him and Itzcoatl of Tenochtitlan bring Maxtla down. He spoke eloquently.

This modern sculpture of Nezahualcoyotl is the work of Mexican
artist Humberto Peraza.

The narrator praised what he accomplished: "Then at last the crimes
of the Tepaneca were clearly seen."[23] The eastern communities joined
the war on the side of the Mexica.

Finally, the bad guys were vanquished. And the star of the
Mexica rose.

Nezahualcoyotl: The Poet King?

Many stories have grown up around Nezahualcoyotl, *tlatoani* of Texcoco. Modern people have wanted to make of him a hero with whom they could identify: an effective warrior, a poet and a musician who abhorred human sacrifice—in other words, a great leader according to today's moral standards. Nezahualcoyotl was indeed a talented and much honored leader of his people. But he attained power and ruled in the ways we would expect a victorious chief of that time and place to have done when we consider the matter realistically.

The military victory that he helped to engineer over Maxtla of Azcapotzalco rendered him a key figure in the new Triple Alliance. The three reigning kings regularly gave their daughters or younger sisters to each other as brides, and Texcoco, on the eastern shore of the lake, also traded actively with the Mexica, so the two ethnic groups were knit together both politically and economically. Nezahualcoyotl increased his power by strategically marrying women from surrounding *altepetls*, raising the sons they bore to be loyal to him, and then sending them back to their mothers' homes to rule. His court was wealthy and large, and in the evenings people gathered to sing and dance and tell histories. Often they mentioned him, or even told the stories from his point of view, for this was the custom.

Nezahualcoyotl featured on Mexico's 100-peso note for thirty years.

One year, these evenings of song provoked a crisis. Nezahualcoyotl had among his women a concubine (or perhaps lesser wife) from Tollan (or Tula). She was a talented singer, and engaged in a sort of flirtatious performative duel with one of Nezahualcoyotl's handsome sons by his primary wife. According to the stories that were told later by Spaniards and those educated by Spaniards, Nezahualcoyotl had to have his son put to death because he had broken the law by betraying him, and this decision—that he was forced to make because of his own laws—made him weep. The tale was evocative of another one the westerners knew well: the story of King Arthur, Lancelot, and Guinevere.

In reality, Nahuatl-language sources teach us that there was another dynamic at play. Nezahualcoyotl was by now an old man, and in the course of his long life, the former Mexica king had died and another had taken his place. Nezahualcoyotl's heirs had been born to him by a close relative of the old Mexica king. Now the new one wanted the rulership of Texcoco to be inherited by one of *his* close connections. He used the theatrical spectacle that had provoked gossip as an excuse to force Nezahualcoyotl's primary wife and her sons out of power, and to replace them with a new primary wife and heirs more sympathetic to him. So it was that when Nezahualcoyotl died in his seventies, with dozens of strapping, grown sons, he was succeeded by a boy of nine, conveniently named Nezahualpilli ("Child of the Hungry One").

Nezahualcoyotl had deftly navigated great political change multiple times in his life. By virtue of being a successful and sometimes ruthless warrior king who interacted astutely with key allies, he had brought the people of Texcoco fifty years of relative stability. Towards the end of his life, he made decisions about the successorship that were necessary in order to prevent trouble with the Mexica, which would have instigated civil war. The Aztecs defined a good king as one who knew when to fight and when not to, who always had his people's long-term good at heart. By those standards, Nezahualcoyotl was indeed a great man.

A RISING POWER

The history of central Mexico in the second half of the fifteenth century is the story of the Mexica triumphing over all challenges and achieving ever greater power. Perhaps not accidentally, this period of a rising tide actually originated in a brutal period of drought and famine, during which the Mexica leaders swore to themselves they would never let the like happen again.

In the memories of the storytellers, the famine, like many catastrophes, had something to do with the year One Rabbit, known to be a carrier of doom. Either the crops had initially failed then, or the famine reached its apogee in that year. In any event, the crops had failed to yield and the earth lay parched and dying. Those who spoke of this period always referenced its horrors. "There was no longer even a bit of a tortilla for sale. The vultures just stood inside the dead bodies and ate of them; no one was burying them anymore."[24] In this time of extreme hardship, some of the Mexica and other peoples of the central valley sold a few of their children to long-distance merchants, who took them away to sell as slaves in distant regions where the rain still fell. "They were brought along by the head," said the storytellers, meaning they were collared by the neck and forced to walk, just like prisoners of war.[25] Such memories were beyond painful.

After these events, the Mexica determined to make more conquests and collect more tribute, in order to inoculate themselves against such disasters in future. A prince named Axayacatl became king in 1469. He was named for a water beetle that flitted easily on the surface of the lake, and indeed he was an expert canoe man and warrior. But it was probably not for such talents that he was chosen.

In fact, his own elder half-brothers by different mothers loved to tell stories about how cowardly he was, needing to buy his prisoners in the slave market since he supposedly never took any on the battlefield.[26] This was almost certainly untrue, but it demonstrates that his merits as a fighter were probably not decisive. Rather, he was the perfect candidate because on his father's side, he was descended of Itzcoatl's branch of the family, and on his mother's, of the main royal line. Thus he brought together two competing lines that might otherwise have ended up fighting.

The plucky water beetle had his work cut out for him in trying to increase Tenochtitlan's wealth and power. He worked hard, leading his people to war personally, and even getting wounded. In the annals of other towns, many of the tribute arrangements they remembered making dated to his rule.[27] Two situations that he had to deal with in quick succession were very serious indeed, and the storytellers spoke of them for generations to come. First, just as he was becoming king, the Mexica were putting to bed a long period of warfare with the Chalca. In an effort to subjugate the people of that community more fully as tribute-payers in the aftermath of the famine, the Mexica had demanded that they send men to help make their main temple grander. This the Chalca refused to do, and it came to war. Eventually exhausted, some Chalca went to sue for peace, but they were rebuffed, and since they were not successful, their people back home decried the very effort they had made, saying no one ever wanted peace with the Mexica anyway. After a few more years of fighting, however, the would-be negotiators were proven right. The Mexica warriors got all the way to the very top of the tallest hill in the area of Chalco, and from there, they were able to "shoot their gods"—that is, to set fire to their temples. This was always the sign

The Curse of the Year One Rabbit

The Aztecs associated the year One Rabbit—which occurred once every fifty-two years—with famine. They even had a saying, "We were one-rabbited," meaning that a calamity of some sort struck. Multiple sets of annals tell us that a terrible drought occurred in the 1450s, culminating in 1454, a year One Rabbit. It long remained an open question as to whether there was an ancient association between that year sign and famine, so that storytellers picked that year of a multi-year disaster to focus on, or whether the horrors of 1454 were so real and so extreme that they for the first time *created* the association in people's minds—which then colored how people told their history in later years, even if it hadn't been told that way before. (For instance, one horrible military defeat that most narrators agreed had occurred in a year Two Reed was occasionally placed in the year One Rabbit. A later historian had simply become convinced that he should put the event in that year.)

In the early 2000s, a group of dendrochronologists (geo-scientists who study tree rings) did a careful study of the matter. There are thirteen One Rabbit years between 882 and 1558, and they found that in central Mexico "ten of these were immediately preceded by below-normal tree growth in the [prior] year Thirteen House".[29]

of utter defeat. If warriors could not prevent this, then they had indeed lost. To top it all off, the Mexica took a royal daughter off to Tenochtitlan, to be a wife to the Mexica tlatoani. Her son would be raised there—and then would return to Chalco to rule, the very worst of situations from a Chalcan point of view.[28]

During these same years, the people of Tlatelolco were growing resentful of their Tenochca brethren. Tlatelolco was a separate settlement at the northern tip of the island, famous for its huge market.

In other words, there was indeed a correlation with drought. This remarkable coincidence would have been more than enough to establish a multi-century connection between the year One Rabbit and famine. The disaster of the mid-1450s would only have dramatized what people already believed.

Representations of the year One Rabbit appear frequently in pre-conquest and early post-conquest art.

Yet the people of Tlatelolco and the people of Tenochtitlan were all Mexica, and were interrelated. They had lived together peacefully for decades, with the larger settlement, Tenochtitlan, calling most of the shots, but with Tlatelolco benefiting from the relationship as well. Then, in the late 1460s, the tlatoani who had ruled Tlatelolco for forty-one years died. He had played a role in the political arrangements made in the region in the aftermath of the Tepaneca wars. His successor, however, did not take the long view. He saw only that Tenochtitlan always got a larger share of the tribute after every military victory.[30]

Moquihuixtli laid plans for war. He did this by contacting numerous city-states and trying to talk them into breaking with the Mexica and coming over to his side when the imminent violence erupted. Just after Chalco's final military defeat he approached them, promising relief from the newly imposed tribute regimen, but they turned him down. One storyteller said that they were so unwilling to risk renewed war that they turned the emissaries over to Axayacatl, who supposedly sacrificed them, had their flesh dumped into a stew, and ordered it served to Moquihuixtli at a state dinner![31] We needn't wonder if the tale is literally true. How could it have been? By the time matters had come to such a head, Moquihuixtli was no longer attending state dinners. But the narrative speaks volumes about Mexica attitudes towards Moquihuixtli's going behind their back to their tributaries. In any event, many communities were likewise offended by Moquihuixtli's approaches, and asked themselves if he would give their lands away when it suited him. One remembered, "He made a promise to Tollan [and other towns], saying, 'When we have defeated our enemy, the Tenochca, I will give you the city of Cuauhtitlan.'"[32] But a few towns were more trusting and did agree to join him when he rose.

The stories told around the evening fires in later years illuminated the deepening political tensions by focusing on Moquihuixtli's marriages. The tlatoani did what kings in his time and place habitually did in such situations: he rearranged his marital relations in order to make a public statement about which alliances he valued and about the succession. He began to insist that his Tenochca wife, Axayacatl's sister, was not his primary consort after all. He insulted her in front of others, calling her thin and unappealing. The young woman, Chalchiuhnenetzin ("Jade Doll"), suffered great humiliations. "She had to sleep among the grinding stones, over in a corner." Worse, her husband grew violent: "He used to really beat her."[33] Some of the stories were quite graphic. In desperation, Chalchiuhnenetzin sent messages to her brother by means of servants. But at first, Axayacatl did not wish to hear her. Perhaps he felt he already had enough problems. Eventually, however, he came to believe her, and signaled that she should come home. Dressed in rags, she made her way back and told her brother everything. "He has given out shields and obsidian-bladed war clubs [to his allies]. I have heard what he says. There are consultations by night.... He says he will destroy us Mexica Tenochca, that the only rulership will be in Tlatelolco."[34]

The Tlatelolcans themselves did not tell stories about this war—barely mentioning it in the histories they recited—for it ended in a great defeat for them. The Tenochca were too powerful, and had too many allies. They ended up victorious, and it was left to them to spin the yarns. The Tlatelolcans attacked first, and with the element of surprise were able to hold their own, in the sense that they were not immediately destroyed. But they were driven back to their part of the island. And later the Tenochca and their allies came en masse in a nearly unstoppable force and literally drove the remaining Tlatelolcan warriors into the lake. Even in the water they continued to chase them, beating the reeds to find those who were hiding. It was later said that the Tenochca "made them quack like ducks." Many were the jokes told by the Tenochca about Tlatelolcan ducks.

A band of warriors chased Moquihuixtli to the top of his people's pyramid temple, and from there he threw himself to the ground. Or perhaps his enemies tossed him down—the storytellers contradicted each other.[35] But in either case, the Tlatelolcans, like the Chalcans, were finished as a great power. From now on, the Mexica's power would be unquestioned. They would consult their allies among the people of Texcoco and Tlacopan—those with whom Itzcoatl had originally made a bid for power—but they would invite few others to their council table.

LATE IMPERIAL CRISES

In the decades just before the Europeans arrived, there was only one remaining city-state in central Mexico powerful enough to resist incorporation into the Mexica sphere. This was Tlaxcala, a large kingdom composed of four separate subunits tightly allied as one in their dealings with outsiders. It lay in the neighboring valley just east of the central basin, around the skirt of a great volcanic mountain, Matlalcueyitl ("Dark Green Skirted One"). The Tlaxcalans had arrived only shortly before the Mexica, so they, too, had all the energy of recently arrived migrants who still remembered their origins very clearly. In about 1510, the Mexica succeeded in winning over one of Tlaxcala's former allies, the town of Huexotzinco. They provided arms and promises of future benefits to the people of Huexotzinco in exchange for their launching a war against Tlaxcala. It did not work out well. The Tlaxcalans told the story with glee: "We pursued them right to their homes and burned their lands."[36] Now starving, many of the Huexotzinca had to march to Tenochtitlan and beg for shelter. They tried to handle the situation by offering one of their noblewomen to the king, Moctezuma, as a wife. But he insulted them by taking her as a concubine.

The Puebla-Tlaxcala valley is dominated by a volcanic mountain once
called Matlalcueyitl, and now La Malinche.

Frustrated by the defeat of the Huexotzinca, the Mexica, including both Tenochca and Tlatelolca warriors, had to pursue the war themselves, and tried make a sneak attack in the dead of night. Again the Tlaxcalans took up the tale:

> Moctezuma ordered that in one single day they would
> surround us and enter secretly to defeat us. He said that he
> would be the jailer [of the Tlaxcalans]. When the invasion
> happened, no one was aware of it [at first]. The people
> were playing the ballgame in Tozcoc before the Tlaxcalan
> rulers. Everyone was there. Yet by evening, the world
> was saying that our enemies had come in order to be
> destroyed.... Uncountable were the lords who died.[37]

Aztec counting markers. These symbols come from tax lists found in the Codex Mendoza; similar ones are found elsewhere. A flag-like figure (*pantli*) represented a group of twenty. Here, ten of these indicate that the people were to give two hundred bundles of cacao. A head of hair (*tzontli*), often illustrated like a feather, symbolized 20 × 20, or 400. Here, two of these indicate that the people are to give 800 conch shells. An ornately decorated bag (*xiquipilli*) represented 400 × 20, or 8,000. Here, three of these indicate that the people are to give a total of 24,000 bunches of colored feathers. Drawings by Gordon Whittaker.

This would matter a great deal in the very near future, for when the Spaniards landed on Mexico's shores about three years later, the Tlaxcalans debated but eventually joined them to bring down the Mexica. But that was in the future.

In the meantime, the Mexica handled defeats like this by exerting power where they could and by spreading stories of their ferocity. For instance, in glyphic histories telling of the dedication of their main temple to Huitzilopochtli in 1487, they sometimes used symbolic numbers meant to evoke a sense of uncountability. They used a base-20 accounting system, and twenty sets of twenty were called (and pictured as) a *centzontli*, referring to a head of hair and eliciting a sense of "almost too many to count." Twenty sets of four hundred (or eight thousand—in practical terms the highest number possible in their world) were called (and pictured as) a *xiquipilli*, a huge sack or purse of precious goods. Thus, in order to emphasize the grandeur of the dedication ceremony, the Mexica said that two or three xiquipilli of captives had been demanded of each of four conquered altepetls, ultimately yielding a collection of more than eighty thousand people who met their deaths on the sacred cutting stone.[38] This number has been repeated by scholars as though it were a literal tally. But it was very obviously a metaphorical statement. Such numbers as "twenty times twenty" or "twenty times four hundred" were regularly used in a symbolic sense. The Aztecs did not have the technological capability to cut the hearts out of eighty thousand people in just a few days; nor would a group that size, larger than the city's population, have allowed them to proceed. Archaeological records demonstrate that far smaller numbers were actually sacrificed under Aztec rule (see Chapter 5).

At the time the Mexica told such stories, their dramatic flair and poetic exaggerations often helped them to frighten others and hence to maintain their power. But of all the stories that they told, this one has undoubtedly hurt them the most ever since. It has been taken as truth, and they have become known as the murderers of tens of thousands. The clearly painted symbols for the numbers (which were easily translated even when other glyphs were becoming hard to understand) and the sensationalistic nature of the statements combined to ensure that although the Mexicas' vibrant and evocative historic tales of political marriages, men, and women would largely be forgotten, this one would live. All the Aztecs were experts at using stories to teach history, to convey the nature of historical predicaments and situations; but in this case, we might say that their approach backfired.

5

TALKING TO THE DIVINE

The tlatoani of Coyoacan, whose name was Tzotzomatzin,
was a *tlamatini* [wise man] as well as a reader of the
stars. When [the Mexica king] Ahuitzotl asked that
[the river] Acuecuexatl be diverted to Mexico, he did
not want to consent. When Ahuitzotl heard the response
of Tzotzomatzin, he thought that he must not want to
release the water. So he called [an adviser], the tlatoani
of Huitzilopochco, whose name was Huitzilatzin. Once
he had arrived in the city, Ahuitzotl revealed to him his
desire to bring the river Acuecuexatl to Tenochtitlan,
and told him also how Tzotzomatzin was saying that if
the Acuecuexatl were diverted to Mexico, it would cause
destruction. Supposedly it was bewitched water, for it had
been enchanted by the great *nahualli* [sorcerer] Cuecuex
who used to bathe there.[1]

Anyone steeped in the Aztec stories recognizes two truths about the
people who told the tales: they were both extremely pragmatic and
highly devout. This seems to have been true of most people who lived
in the past, so perhaps the Aztecs were no exception. Their storytellers were themselves aware of a certain tension regarding this issue.
Tzotzomatzin, whose name meant "Honored Old Rag," had all the
qualities of a beloved old and useful piece of cloth. He responded in

just the right way to different situations. Of course he did not want to divert water from his people's lands to those of the Mexica. Who would want such a thing?! At the same time, he probably really did have great respect for the powers of the old sorcerer Cuecuex, who had been among the founders of his community and had a special relationship with the river. The teller of the tale implied that both were true—that Tzotzomatzin was both practical and devout. Yet there is no question that Tzotzomatzin used the story of Cuecuex to try to save his people's water, and there is likewise no question that Ahuitzotl's adviser assumed that this was the only truth:

> When Huitzilatzin heard [Tzotzomatzin's objections],
> he said to the tlatoani Ahuitzotl, "O lord king, who says
> that the [river] Acuecuexatl wouldn't be able to come?
> Isn't Tzotzomatzin just making fun of you? Maybe he
> doesn't want to give you this water because it lies in his
> lands. Of course the water can come to Tenochtitlan!"
> Then Ahuitzotl got angry and gave orders to go strangle
> and kill Tzotzomatzin—who had spoken prudently.
> So they brought [the waters of] the Acuecuexatl to the
> city. But the water rose with such force that it flooded
> the city and people fled. And when the city flooded,
> Ahuitzotl was equally angry with Huitzilatzin, and he
> gave orders to go and strangle and kill him, too. Thus
> it was done, for he had spoken falsely. So it was that
> two kings were killed because of the Acuecuexatl.

From this story, one might conclude that the Aztecs were eminently practical, even cynical, more than they were devout. Tzotzomatzin

"Water brought from the springs of Coyoacan to Tenochtitlan."
An Indigenous artist created this drawing for fray Diego Durán's
volume, *History of the Indies of New Spain.*

was willing to use a story of a sorcerer to try to save his people's water supply; Huitzilatzin was willing to dismiss such stories out of hand in order to flatter and support the high king. But the narrator gives divinity the last word. In the end, both of the two lesser kings who had tried to get their own way died because of the power of the spirit-infused river.

The Aztecs as they went about their daily activities often found themselves caught up in this very issue, this tension between their human desire to try to gain their own ends as they proceeded through life and their equally human belief that it was not they who were ultimately in control. They believed in the power of the divine universe, and while they sometimes experienced awe and reverence, they often simply felt buffeted and vulnerable. They didn't like such feelings, and in their songs often called out angrily to the gods: "You laugh at us! You think nothing of us. You kill us, destroy us."[2] They were not willing to give in completely to such emotions, to go down without a fight, so to speak. On the contrary, they seemed to take it as a challenge to find ways to mitigate their vulnerability, to forge some semblance of control, albeit in small ways.

To do this they relied on various kinds of ritual specialists, on people whose lives were devoted to learning to communicate with the divine. A great deal has been written about such matters by scholars relying on statements left to us by Spaniards, or elicited from Indigenous people by Spaniards. Such accounts are often contradictory. Matters become clearer when we listen only to what the Nahuas had to say when they were speaking to each other. There were numerous words for spiritually powerful people, and the nuances are often lost on us today. But certain patterns are distinguishable in the Nahuatl sources. It seems that there were three types of specialists, that is, people who made their livings by intervening with the divine. There was the *ticitl*, the doctor, who helped to cure bodily illnesses. There was the *tonalpouhqui*, the soothsayer, summoned when it was necessary to assess which day or days looked to be fortuitous when an event was planned. And there was the *tlamacazqui*, the priest, who served in the pyramid temples, keeping the fires lit and performing other ceremonies.

Each of these could be male or female, old or young, noble or commoner, and each could also be a nahualli, or sorcerer, someone so in tune with the spiritual power of the universe as to read its workings and cast spells, possibly even with the ability to temporarily take another shape. It was also possible to be a nahualli without being a doctor or soothsayer or temple priest. A chief could sometimes have the power of a nahualli. An ordinary farmer who was especially devout and wise could become one, as could his wife. It was, in short, a personal characteristic, not a job description.

The Myth of the *Tlamatini*

The word *tlamatini* means "knowledgeable one," and the Aztecs applied it to various kinds of people. Yet in western scholarship, it has long been used to refer to cloaked philosophers who produced poetry and religious texts to provide moral guidance to their people. There never were any such figures—and yet we must not rush to judge those who promoted the idea. It all began not long after the conquest, when the Franciscan Bernardino de Sahagún spent decades working on the Florentine Codex. He was well aware of the condescension and hostility evinced by many Spaniards toward Indigenous people, and he knew from experience how wrongheaded such views were. He made it his life's work to record the Nahuas' culture, editing along the way as he saw fit. He expressed true respect for the complex philosophy and depth of feeling found in their songs, stories, and prayers, comparing their work to that of the ancient Greeks.

In the 1950s, a great Mexican academic, Miguel León-Portilla, likewise battled against the prejudices of his era. He had an abiding respect for what the Aztecs had accomplished and he wished to bring their voices "within hearing distance of the rest of the world,"[3]

The same was true of the quality of a tlamatini (literally, "knowledgeable one"). The tlamatini have often been described in western scholarly literature as "wise men" or "holy men," with many attendant virtues. But the Nahuatl-language texts use the word to describe any of the specialists: a particularly good doctor, soothsayer, or temple priest could be said to be a tlamatini. Someone who was none of these things could also be a tlamatini. Tzotzomatzin, the tlatoani of Coyoacan, was described thus because in his years as a chief he had handled so many situations so well and was good at reading the stars.

We do not have detailed information, but we can glean some important truths about each of the three social roles that we know proving that the Aztecs had not just thoughts, but philosophy. He, too, put the matter in terms that he thought his readers would understand. "Among the Nahuas, then, as among the Greeks, it was the lyric poets who first became aware of and enunciated the great problems of human existence."[4] As the world's interest in disempowered peoples grew in the 1960s and 1970s, León-Portilla's work was translated into many languages. It did the work on behalf of the Aztecs' reputation that he hoped it would. In his book and in the works of others that followed, it was a small step to move from discussing philosophy to discussing philosophers; elaborate descriptions of the *tlamatinime* (plural of tlamatini) were created by those who did not have full access to Nahuatl sources. Those who passed on the notion of Aztec wise men resembling Socrates or Christian friars could not possibly have had better intentions, yet they were not being true to Nahua traditions. Today, scholars in Mexico are launching new studies of the Aztecs, more deeply based in Indigenous language and culture, bringing the conversation forward in ways that undoubtedly would have made both Sahagún and León-Portilla proud.

existed. Let us take them each in turn. First, the most typical ticitl (doctor) was in fact a woman, and the most typical patient was a woman giving birth. In such contexts, translators often use the word "midwife," but in the actual texts, the gender-neutral word remains the same, ticitl: "The doctor (ticitl) fired, heated the *temazcalli* (the sweat bath), where she massaged the pregnant woman's abdomen; she placed it [the fetus] correctly. She kept turning it as she massaged her, as she went on manipulating her."[5]

Doctors were involved in all health crises, not just childbirth. In the Florentine Codex, the Spanish questioners and editors tried to draw a distinction between a doctor who did what European doctors did ("a good doctor")—lancing infections, purging the intestines, providing salves for hemorrhoids, setting bones, massaging sore muscles, providing herbs to lower fever—and a doctor who was a nahualli and used sorcery or cast fortune-telling stones to determine what treatment to offer ("a bad doctor").[6] In the Aztec world, however, these figures would undoubtedly have been one and the same. A trusted and experienced doctor might well cast stones for reassurance before she (or he) began the work of setting a bone, for instance.

The only doctors whom the Nahuatl-language sources allow us to know intimately are the midwives, who helped birthing women endure a crisis that was both bodily and spiritual: rather than simply bringing the infant through the birth canal, they were understood to be aiding a mother to go out into the universe in a racking, spiritual quest and capture a new soul for this world. They knew more than contemporary European doctors did about what we would call the relevant medical issues, in that they valued cleanliness and believed in the need to encourage the child-bearer: "My daughter, exert yourself! What shall we do with you? Here are those who have become your mothers. This is your task. Seize well the little shield. My daughter, my youngest one, you are a warrior woman. Face it, that is, bear down, imitate the warrior woman [the goddess] Cihuacoatl Quilaztli!"[7] But a good midwife also believed in forces beyond her control, in the overwhelming power of the divine, and she prayed to many gods or goddesses, beginning with Quetzalcoatl and Quilaztli and sometimes ending with Chalchiuhtlicue, the water goddess, as she bathed the infant.

Like the doctors, the soothsayers played an essential role in society. They were the keepers and interpreters of painted books

A woman doctor (*ticitl*) helps a patient to give birth (Florentine Codex).

of the ritual calendar, consisting of twenty groups of thirteen days, or 260 separate day signs, each with its own known characteristics. The soothsayers' most important work occurred when a child was born, and they were needed to interpret the baby's fate. They were also called upon to offer prognostications when other important events were planned, such as a wedding or the launching of a merchant expedition. Their words brought great comfort. When a trading expedition was to be launched, for instance, the soothsayers would help a merchant family pick a suitable day for their son and his companions and slaves to set out with their bundles of goods, so that they could feel confident in offering encouragement and hope: "These are the words of advice with which I strengthen you, my child. As I am your mother, your father, so you have me as your protector, your comforter. You are suffering as you stand up and leave the altepetl, your home. You are about to leave your relatives, you are about to abandon your home, your house, the resting place of your head, your childhood crib. Already you meet [the day] One Serpent.… You suffer, my child, young man. Exert all your strength.

Welcoming a New Baby

Every time a baby was born in the Nahua world, it was a joyous occasion. The Florentine Codex recounts the prayers offered by a Mexica midwife at the birth:

> When the baby had arrived on earth, then the midwife shouted. She gave war cries, which meant that the honored woman had fought a good battle, had become a brave warrior, had taken a captive, had captured a baby [from the universe].
>
> Then the midwife spoke to the baby.... "You have suffered exhaustion, you have suffered fatigue [meaning, Welcome!], my youngest one, my precious child, precious necklace, precious quetzal feather. You have arrived. Rest, find repose. Here are gathered your beloved grandfathers, your beloved grandmothers, who were awaiting you. Here into their hands you have arrived. Do not sigh! Do not be sad! Why have you come, why have you been brought here? It is true that you will endure the sufferings of hardship and fatigue, for our lord has ordered, has disposed that there will be pain, affliction, and misery [in our lives on earth]. There will be work, labor for morning and evening sustenance. [But] there is sweat, weariness and labor where there is to be eating, drinking, and the wearing of [beautiful] clothing. Welcome!"
>
> And the midwife right away cut the baby's umbilical cord and took it. She removed that which is called the afterbirth in which the baby came wrapped, in which it came enveloped. This she buried in a corner of the house. But the baby's umbilical cord was saved. It was dried out, and [that of a boy] was left in a battlefield.[8]

Where will you wander? Will you die? May the tears and sympathy of your elders go with you as reward and recompense, to gird and clothe you. For thus did your elders also go."[9]

The word most often used for priest, tlamacazqui, literally translates "one who gives things"—meaning, in this case, one who tends to the gods. Priests lived in the pyramid temples to which they were dedicated. They swept before dawn and brought what was needed to the altars. During the day, they did whatever work was needed— carting wood, making adobe for a building, cultivating the temple's crops, or digging a canal. Every evening they performed the holy rite of auto-sacrifice, bleeding themselves with thorns from the maguey (tequila) plant:

> When still a little light shone, or when it was already becoming dark, it was the time of the cutting of the maguey spines. When it was quite dark, when it was already deep night, then the priests began what was called the placing of the maguey spine. One at a time they went forth. First each bathed himself. Then they took their shell trumpets, and incense ladles, sacks filled with incense, and they took up pine torches. Thereupon each set forth to place the maguey thorns. They went naked. Those who would perform a great penance might go as far as two leagues to place the maguey spine—maybe into the woods, or the dry flatlands, or the waters. A younger one went perhaps half a league to place the spines. Each bore his shell trumpet and went blowing it. Wherever he came to be, he went blowing a trumpet.[10]

After the conquest, when Spaniards asked Indigenous people to describe the priests as a group, they spoke of them reverently. Yet when they spoke of them unselfconsciously, in unguarded moments,

The Codex Borgia served as a guidebook for priests. Here, we see a classic central Mexican image of a palace or temple.

they remembered them as people whom they had not always liked. The priests were the teachers at the *calmecac*, the school for future priests, and many of the young boys from noble families who later worked with the Spanish friars were related to older men who had once attended the school. They remembered, for instance, that a rambunctious boy could be punished on a certain festival day with being violently submerged under water in the most terrifying way. Sometimes things went too far and a boy actually died. If a family feared this might well happen to their boy, they could try bribing

In this illustration, also from the Codex Borgia, we find a map of a complex ceremony featuring flint knives.

his priestly teachers with gifts of wild turkeys and other delicacies, which often worked to temper the castigation.[11]

NEGOTIATING WITH DIVINITY

What is striking about the stories involving all these ritual specialists is how often kings and other leaders disputed with them. They argued with them about their conclusions, and if they had been convinced, sometimes sought to negotiate with them about what course was to be taken. Fatalistic these leaders may have been on one level, but on another level, they were anything but. One lord might settle in a certain altepetl, learning to "care for its traditions," because they were willing to name him a god-bearing priest; another tlatoani might leave his community because of a huge fight he had with the priests within his own calpolli, in which he ended up killing some of them.[12]

Such stories could be just as poetic and suggestive as those on any other theme. Our old friend King Coxcox of Culhuacan had a grandson, we remember, who came to visit him when he grew up. He greeted him happily: "Welcome, my child. It is true I lost a daughter [years ago], from whom you have sprung. Sit down, for you are my grandson. Such as I am, I am old and must die. Here in Culhuacan it is you who will be the ruler [someday]." The boy's answer did not come as the old man would have wished:

> That Iztactototl ["White Turkey"], he was a little like a
> reader of the stars, the way he spoke. After hearing the
> words [of his grandfather], he said nothing. Eventually
> the ruler Coxcox went inside. Then from within the
> house he sent a messenger to inform him that he was
> not to come again, and he was also told that he would
> definitely become ruler, succeeding his grandfather.
> When Iztactototl heard those words, he laughed and said,
> "Whose ruler would I be? For the Culhuacan altepetl is
> not to endure. It is to crumble and disperse. But I say give
> this message to the king, my grandfather. It will probably
> not happen in his lifetime, and when it does, some

could go to our home [in Cuauhtitlan] and become our
followers there.[13]

Coxcox was not cowed by the oracular mutterings of his divinely
inspired grandson. He angrily demanded evidence: "That little
boy, that child, what is he saying?! Ask him what it is that would
destroy our altepetl and who would destroy it? Is this a death that
is not from here [of this world]? How would it rise against us? Pox,
diarrhea, coughing, fever, consumption exist, and we know that
the sun might be eaten [in an eclipse] and the earth might shake,
and we might have to sacrifice people. But how is our altepetl to be
crumbled and dispersed?!" The boy explained that he saw a time
coming soon when many small problems would beset the altepetl
and the people would have to disperse to make their own way, but
his grandfather was far from convinced.

Sometimes arguments between a lord and a priest could be downright frightening. One narrator recounted an exchange between the
high king Moctezuma and one of the "skull-rack lords," the priests
who tended the *tzompantli*, the rack upon which the craniums of
sacrifice victims were mounted. Moctezuma was so enraged at one
of the priest's predictions that he had the man killed:

The reason the skull-rack lord met his death is that
he had answered back to Moctezuma—who had asked
him how things should be done, saying, "As I see it, the
house [temple] of Huitzilopochtli should be gold, and
the inside should be jade, with quetzal feathers. In fact,
it would require tribute from everywhere, so that it might
be used for our god. What do you think?" At that, the

skull-rack lord answered him, saying, "O lord, o ruler,
no! Understand that by so doing you would invite the
destruction of your altepetl and offend the heavens. For we
are being watched here. You must understand—that one
[Huitzilopochtli] is not going to be our god [in future].
There is the creator and owner of all things. He comes."
Hearing this, Moctezuma was enraged. He said to the
skull-rack lord, "Go, and await my word." Thus died
the skull-rack lord and all his children.[14]

Still, though the king had the last word in the story, once again, the
narrator was subtly reminding his audience that it was the man
who could speak to divinity and grasp its messages who turned out
to be right in the long run. By the time the speaker told this story,
a generation after conquest, Huitzilopochtli was in fact no longer
the people's god—at least not their primary one.

Yet if the bards felt they needed to remind their listeners that it
was not wise to ignore signs and signals given by the divine, it may
have been because so many people devoted a great deal of time
and energy to finding work-arounds. Indeed, in the case of the
tonalpouhque, the soothsayers, helping people to do this very thing
was sometimes their primary duty. An infant was to be ceremonially bathed on the day it arrived, or else four days hence, and then
receive that day as his or her name day. But if a child were born
on an inauspicious day, and four days later was the same or worse,
the soothsayer could help the family find a reason to ceremonially
welcome a child on some other day that would bring better fortune:
"They sent for the soothsayer. They sent for him the instant the baby
arrived, the instant it had been born. He opened up and looked

158

at the red-and-the-black [the writings]. He inquired if it was during the night that it was born, if it had arrived, perhaps, at the division of the night [midnight], or perhaps when the division of the night had passed." Fudging on whether a child had been born before or after midnight (or experiencing genuine uncertainty on that matter) often gave people better options. But sometimes the news was still dismal. "Then the soothsayer chose a good day, not just the fourth day after, for it to be bathed. He skipped more, seeking a good day to be governed by, a good one of its near companions." For making this adjustment the specialist was richly rewarded. "Not just a little did they give him. He went away with turkeys and a load of food."[15]

It is easy to see the temptation to try to amend a baby's fate. Sometimes the signs were so bad that one had very little to lose. If a girl were born on the day One House, for instance, her very life might be at stake. It wasn't just that she would probably prove to be unskilled at women's work—though it was feared she would—but worse, she might find herself sold as a slave and face the cutting stone. It was unthinkable to accept this possibility without at least trying to help. And four days later was Four Death, hardly an improvement. "In order to improve her day somewhat, they bathed her on Three Serpent, for the reason given about all days numbered Three [that they were of good fortune]. Pulling one day, they made it good." If the family were real risk-takers, they could push matters even further. "And if perhaps they should wish it, they could bathe her later, on Seven Water, because of the goodness of each day sign with the number Seven."[16] The fourth book of the twelve-book Florentine Codex was essentially a day-by-day guide to the calendar, as explained by a knowledgeable tonalpouhqui. Over and over, the speaker explained what adjustments had to be made in certain cases.

The same principle seems to have applied to other kinds of omens as well. On the one hand, the people felt themselves surrounded by signs from the divine universe, signs which they believed fervently they needed to heed. These beliefs were durable. Towards the end of the 1500s, when the people were theoretically Christian, someone in the Puebla-Tlaxcala valley, just east of Mexico City, remembered that in the year 1546, a wall of snake-like clouds had appeared to run repeatedly across the sky, just before a terrible epidemic broke out. The implication was that it had been an omen. The exact words incorporated the name of the god Mixcoatl ("Cloud Snake"). The literal translation of the text would be: "This was when Mixcoatl ran by [repeatedly], hanging from the sky."[17]

Yet within that context, it is notable that the Aztecs' explanations of the old omens regularly included commentary as to how the universe was in fact offering a warning about a fate that could yet be avoided if one paid attention and acted in accordance. For example, it was a portent of disaster if a skunk entered a household compound, especially if he let loose his foul odor; it was therefore of the utmost importance that no one spit at it, or chase it, or do anything that might provoke it. Children were warned about this lest there be any mistake. If a group of travelers heard a white-hooded owl make its unearthly cry, an omen of death, they collected together at the foot of a tall tree and bound together all their walking staves, "which represented the god Yiacateuctli [lord of leadership]." Then "before him, they did penance, bled themselves, cut their ears and drew straws through." Having done that together, they mastered some of their fear, and thus often found they had no problem at all. On certain nights, it was known that malevolent forces walked the earth, for instance, the *cihuapipiltin*, the raging, miserable spirits of women who had died in childbirth. It was best to stay inside at those times. If a pregnant woman absolutely had to go out then or on other dangerous evenings, she could reduce the risk by carrying a small bag of ash at her breast. If one was being pursued by a nahualli, or sorcerer, and it was feared that he might enter the household in some magical disguise, the answer was to lay a shining obsidian knife in a bowl of water. Like Quetzalcoatl in the old story,[18] when he looked into the shimmering mirror, he would see his true reflection, including the reflection of his own evil intent, and he would feel powerful emotions and never try to harm the pursued again.[19]

CEREMONIES OF SACRIFICE

A central element in any consideration of Aztec people's attempts to communicate with divinity must be their relationship to the ceremonies of human sacrifice. In its original formulation, the idea of giving up a human life in gratitude to the gods was well within the typical range of human spiritual beliefs, as we saw in Chapter 2. But something significant did change over the course of the later decades of the fifteenth century. By then, the Mexica political elite— the extended families constituting the governing class—ruled over a vast territory containing a wide array of peoples who were forced to pay substantial tribute. Though many chiefly families in these far-flung villages were tightly allied with them, many others resented them. The Mexica and their closest allies had no special weapons that no one else could access, so they were indeed vulnerable. They dealt with this by turning human sacrifice into a horrendous—and effective—political tool. They were quite blunt about this, explaining

Visitors speak to the Mexica high king about potential warfare.
From Diego Durán, *History of the Indies of New Spain*.

that when they wished to take over a new territory and a war for it had begun, they would kidnap a few young men from that area, bring them to the city "as Moctezuma's guests" to watch the worst of the ceremonies, and then let them return home. The Mexica were confident that they would tell their people that it was not worth the risk to try to ally with neighbors and attempt to prevent a take-over, for if they lost the result would be horrific beyond words. "In this way they were undone and disunited," brusquely added the Mexica commentator.[20]

The ceremonies had indeed grown to be terrifying. The Mexica celebrated according to the same ceremonial calendar as all other Nahuas in their region, but they now had the power and capacity to kill many prisoners, in numbers they could not have dreamed of not so long ago, when they themselves were vulnerable wanderers. The solar calendar consisted of eighteen months of twenty days each, followed by five days of uncertainty while the world waited for the year to begin anew. In each of these months at least one person was killed in a religious festival, and often many more. The first two months of the year were the most terrible of all. In the first, Quauitl Eua ("Rain Departs"), at the start of the dry season, a mammoth debt was paid to the universe: small children were killed. In the processions, they came crying, and today their bones show that they were malnourished. (Had they come from impoverished war-torn regions? Or had they been kept prisoner?) In the second month, Tlacaxipeualiztli ("Flaying of Men"), dozens of captive warriors were killed in a gruesome gladiatorial spectacle that had been designed in the time of Moctezuma the First, in the period of the Mexicas' great expansion in the 1460s.[21] The great pyramid ran with blood.

In certain ceremonies, it was a woman or women who had to die. Sometimes these girls and young women, so far from home, kept up a stoical front, like their warrior brothers. But not always. "Some, in truth, wept," remembered one man years later.[22] Sometimes they died in ignorance of what was to happen. In the eleventh month, Ochpaniztli ("Sweeping of the Road"), women healers—again, the word ticitl, doctor—surrounded an unsuspecting prisoner of war who had been kept for the purpose, and arrayed her as the goddess Toci ("Our Grandmother"). For this ritual, it was supposed to be important that the victim not sob or grieve, so the celebrants deceived her:

They said to her: "My daughter, now at last the king,
Moctezuma, will sleep with you. Be happy." They did not
let her know that she was going to die, for in truth she was
to die unaware. They adorned and completely arrayed her.
When it was the middle of the night, they brought her [to

The Ballgame

All over Mesoamerica, people made balls out of the sap of the rubber tree. The Aztecs called rubber *olin* from the verb *olini* ("to move"). They loved the nature of the small black balls that soared and bounced and almost seemed to hold motion within them once set off by even the smallest push. The rules of the ballgame varied regionally. Among the Aztecs, an aerial view of the stone court generally looked like a traditional capital "i" (I), but inside the main court, what mattered to the players were not the pockets at the end, but rather, the slanting walls on the two long sides, whitewashed and smooth, at the top of each of which was set a stone hoop. Teams of two (or sometimes three) men had to keep the ball in play without using their hands. They used their upper arms, thighs, waists, and even buttocks, and if they got the ball through the hoop, they won.

The game had sacred symbolism, but different people described its significance differently. Many agreed it was connected to the movement of celestial orbs in the heavens, but there was also widespread association between the ball and the power of the human skull. (In fact, that connection existed beyond Mexico, among Indigenous peoples far to the north.[23]) Games began with prayers on the part of priests. There were apparently occasions when the losers—or other chosen victims—were sacrificed to the gods, but from what we can glean, that was relatively rare. Two generations after the conquest, the Indigenous writer Chimalpahin expressed his frustration at having been unable to verify when (or if) this really happened.[24] Off-handed references to the game in

the temple]. Then none spoke, none talked, none coughed. It was as if the earth lay dead, late at night. And everyone gathered round in the darkness. And when they came to the place where she was to die, then they seized her. One took her up on his back, and they suddenly cut off her head.[26]

German artist Christoph Weiditz sketched some visiting Aztecs who were demonstrating their ballgame at the Spanish royal court in 1529.

various annals indicate that it was primarily a form of entertainment, beloved of nobles and commoners alike. What was at stake most of the time was not anyone's life, but rather, the extensive bets that had been placed of cloaks, gold, and other goods. A great deal of wealth could change hands in a day, as they played round after round, with different players and teams cycling through. Moctezuma was said to have loved the game, and he happily took the Spaniards to see it.[25]

The descriptions of the ceremonies found in the Florentine Codex are agonizingly hard to read. They were elicited by Spanish friars, intent on demonstrating the evils of the prior regime, and they are effective. But pulling back and considering, we realize there is much they do not tell us. We are not told how many died or how many witnessed

Painting from the Historia Tolteca Chichimeca commemorating a ritual ballgame played by the Chichimecs in preparation for their war in Cholula. At bottom, we see an aerial view of the ballcourt. Above, we find a *chinampa* filled not with crops, but with fire and water, which together symbolize battle.

the deaths; nor are we told much about what the people who were *not* specialists involved in the ceremonies thought or felt about what they witnessed. Certainly political and military leaders relied on the ceremonies of sacrifice; professionally invested priests developed a sort of cult around them. But how did they affect most people?

For the first question—as to how many people were likely killed by the Mexicas' state-sponsored priestly hierarchy during the late imperial era—we can turn to archaeology for help. In the 1970s, Mexico launched an extraordinary archaeological investigation dedicated to the excavation and study of the great Aztec temple (Templo Mayor) just off Mexico City's main plaza, near today's cathedral. Over the course of the first four decades, they found a total of about four hundred and fifty skulls throughout the complex. This number seemed surprisingly small, considering the statements made by the Spaniards as well as those elicited by them. No one had found anything resembling the *huey tzompantli*, the "great skull rack," a hideous tower of death spoken of in a number of the sources. Then in 2015 it at last came to light. The structure has proven to contain at least another six hundred and fifty crania. Even if we assume that the skulls toward the top were destroyed by the Spaniards when they knocked the thing down, and that others had simply crumbled before the tower was buried, we cannot imagine a total of more than about a thousand in the edifice.[27] There is supposed to have been a second tower, so let us say we are now looking at two thousand skulls. When we consider that this was the result of decades of sacrifice ceremonies, there seems to be no alternative other than to lower considerably our estimates of how many people were actually killed every year. And indeed, a much lower number fits with common sense: the Mexica did not have the technological capability to kill tens of thousands of people and dispose of them in short order. In one set of historical annals, a detail appears that is probably quite illuminating. In the bundling of fifty-two years that occurred in 1507, the two most powerful kings, Moctezuma of Tenochtitlan and Nezahualpilli of Texcoco, each committed themselves to giving an impressive twenty sacrifice victims.[28] It is dreadful to think of those forty people going to their deaths, but it is a far cry from imagining that it was four hundred, or four thousand, or even forty thousand. It seems we have let our imaginations—or the conquering Spaniards' imaginations—run away with us.

What regular folk in the city made of matters is a question that is much harder to address: no exciting new archaeological discovery will be able to help us here. There are contextual layers that we must take into consideration before we try to address it. First, there is ample evidence that the Aztecs in general and the Mexica specifically bemoaned death and loved life. Their songs mourn the inescapability of death, the tragedy that each person's time on earth is in effect "borrowed," to use their word. Their admonitions to their children were all about fighting for life, both their own and their people's. Their stories demonstrate discomfort with sacrifice in particular. Some of the characters who face the fire or the cutting stone rage, and some cry. We have seen one victim swear that her people's descendants will avenge her, and parents swear that they will free their daughters taken for sacrifice. Significantly, sometimes even those who commit the sacrifice live to regret it. In one ancient tale, captives were taken, and some women told them, "We are going to Tollan now. You will go with us, and when we get there, we will use you to make a celebration."[29] Only when it was too late did the women learn that the tied-up and costumed figures were their own husbands!

The skull rack (*tzompantli*) at the Templo Mayor in Tenochtitlan.

Second, the Indigenous people whom the Spaniards questioned offered a great deal of unsolicited information about what they remembered of the religious holidays of their youths, and it often wasn't human sacrifice. These other elements were often not the ones that the friars were interested in, but they were nevertheless what came out in bits and pieces, despite being asked about other things. It seems that Aztec young people were very much like other young people around the world: They remembered the joy and excitement of special holy days. They spoke of the looping garlands of flowers, and the tamales and other delicious holiday foods that the women prepared. On certain days, relatives greeted children in the extended family by briefly picking them up by their heads, saying they needed to let their bodies stretch out so they would grow! They all laughed at the memory of "casting bags" in the seventeenth month: everybody made little woven bags out of dried plant fibers and then filled them with tiny flowers or bits of paper or leaves pressed into balls. (Naughty little boys had to be watched, so that they wouldn't fill their bags with small stones.) Then it was time to wait for unwary passers-by and throw the bags at any who appeared. Boys looked for pretty girls. On most holidays there were bonfires, with shell trumpets sending out their haunting calls. People danced, sometimes for hours. Often they had exotic costumes or extraordinary decorations. Some even brought along flying birds tied to rods. A few people could thrill everybody else by eating live snakes or frogs.[30]

None of this seems like a description of people who are shortly going to watch the ritual murder of another human being (or multiple human beings). And yet that is what happened, at least for some of the people some of the time. The descriptions of the ceremonies make it clear that there were always audiences, in some months large, in others small. The watchers were not shrieking and trembling as if at a massive orgy, as modern movies would have us believe: they were sober, even somber, sometimes carrying certain flowers, sometimes dancing majestically. The warriors who had taken the prisoners who were to die had a special relationship with them. In some ceremonies they spoke to them beforehand; always they kept their remains with them in their homes in a special reed chest until they themselves died. Still, no matter how respectful—even grateful—the celebrants seem to have been, the fact remains that watching such killings would have affected people if they saw them month after month. All humans become desensitized to violence and even to snuffing out life if they are exposed often enough. Yet the Nahuatl-language sources do not bring us face to face with cruel or desensitized people.

Perhaps most people were not called upon to go often. We cannot know. Nor can we know with certainty what may have been meant by allusions to the victims' blood being "eaten" in the households of the warriors who had taken them prisoner. Perhaps we should take seriously the statement of one man who described what happened very explicitly, referring to the period right before conquest: "When they had cut open the slave or captive's breast, then [the bringer of the victim] took his or her blood in a vessel, and then would cast a paper into the vessel, which drew up the blood. Then he carried it in the vessel, and placed upon the lips of all the Devils [god images] the blood of the person who had died for the gods."[31] In short, in this man's memory, they touched the blood to the lips of statues. On another occasion, when they spoke of eating the god Huitzilopochtli, it turned out they meant that they broke up and ate a giant bread-statue or cake made of amaranth flour and decorated to look like the god rather than a human being dressed like him.[32]

In the mid-sixteenth century, the overall impression given by most people who still remembered the ceremonies seems to have been a mournful sadness; in their words they evinced no shame, no stony coldness, no hideous joy. Texts mentioning religious ceremonies speak of the mournful, powerful music of the conch shells calling out to people. Other sources mention calling up the wind at religious ceremonies, and ceramic instruments have been found, which, when played by skilled musicians, do indeed recreate the sound of wind and storms. These small artifacts have been called "death whistles" in modern times, and some people love to assert that they must have been used to create a shrieking noise just as

CHAPTER 5

Conch Shells

Archaeologists have found shells of many kinds from both
the Atlantic and the Pacific in what was once Tenochtitlan. They
were brought as part of tribute payments and in the packs of long-
distance merchants. Shells were symbolic of water and of life, clear
manifestations of the divine. They made for beautiful jewelry, and
could be used to decorate other objects as well. The Mexica seem
to have loved the conch shell most of all. Carvings of conches lie
along Tlaloc's pyramid in the great temple, and a cross-section of
the conch is associated with Quetzalcoatl. The people's special
reverence for this particular shell might have been due to the
fact that in addition to their visual appeal conches also produced
haunting, beautiful music, used to call the people to gatherings.
A shell that could do this was called a *quiquiztli*, a conch trumpet.
Later, when the Spaniards arrived with their cannons and muskets,
the people struggled to find a name for an object that produced
such a remarkable sound and light show. They came up with
tlequiquiztli, "fire conch."

This conch-shell trumpet has a carefully etched design showing a dancing
singer with speech scrolls coming from his mouth. The work was probably
done in Mexico's southern or central highlands by a Maya or Mixtec artist.

someone was about to die, in an effort to deepen the terror further. But no one, Spaniard or Nahua, wrote anything like that in the sixteenth century.

Still, we must circle back to the ultimate question. We can never know how many Mexica went to see the ceremonies, or how often, or exactly what they were thinking and feeling, but we do know that their ceremonial lives revolved around the knowledge that human sacrifice was occurring on a larger scale than ever before, and that they each had at least an occasional sight of it. We also know that many people were aware of the precariousness of Tenochtitlan's political dominance of the region, and of the resulting need to frighten others into submission, lest they themselves be captured and killed. And we know that at the same time, they deeply believed in the need to express their gratitude to the divine universe for its many gifts to humanity by means of the ultimate sacrifice—life itself. The people seem to have allowed their world view and their desires and fears concerning their own futures to build on and support each other—and to smother inconvenient questions that their subconscious minds might have raised. If that is correct, the Aztecs were not the first people—and were far from the last—to have done such a thing. Do not many of us believe what it is most convenient for us to believe a great deal of the time, choosing to see and not to see as best suits us? Perhaps we should consider carefully the many other facets of the Aztecs' lives before we presume to judge all of them harshly. Their predicament was far from simple.

6

ADAPTING TO A NEW WORLD

Right at 7 o'clock began an eclipse of God the universal ruler's sun. The prediction and decree of the scholar came true. When 9 o'clock arrived, it got completely dark; it resembled 7 o'clock in the evening, and for a good quarter of an hour darkness lingered, and the little birds, the crows, the buzzards, all fell on the ground and went about fluttering and making very mournful cries. And something like yellow tassels of flame spread over [Mount] Popocatepetl. Something like the smoke of flames was on it. Then it was as if people lost their senses; some ran to church; some kept falling in their terror; but only three died right then. At the time nothing but weeping reigned. People no longer recognized each other [in the darkness]. And then everywhere the bells tolled in all the churches. Only at the cathedral and [the friary of] San Francisco did the bells not ring, because the lord bishop did not wish it, because many people would die [in the resulting panic]. Right at 10 o'clock it got light. What was blocking the sun was just a black being. When he left the sun behind, everyone saw how he left it behind and went falling on [Mount] Maltalcueye, how what was blocking the sun then appeared facing North.

Annals of Puebla, 1691

Christian religious stories or myths began to arrive in Mexico in 1521. At that point, Spaniards had already been exploring Mexico's coastline for two decades, and had been present in and around Tenochtitlan for two years while they waged war against the Mexica. But it was only after 1521 that enough Spaniards settled and began to interact regularly with Indigenous people as to be able to convey their religious stories successfully to significant numbers of people. Then began a fascinating period during which Indigenous people had to contrive to come to terms with overlapping sets of beliefs. The process took many generations, and many Mexicans insist that it is still ongoing.

Yet for many years, this subject was not studied, partly because so many Europeans and Euro-descended people were invested in believing a fanciful story or myth of their own about what the Indigenous people purportedly told themselves at the moment of contact. The conquerors insisted that the Indigenous people had mistaken Hernando Cortés for the god Quetzalcoatl, according to the terms of an ancient prophecy. Moctezuma had therefore immediately turned his kingdom over to the newcomers, who in short order taught the bedazzled people to worship the Christian God. It was a tale flattering to the Spaniards, and by extension, to any people of European descent.

What really happened was quite different. When Moctezuma's vassals arrived from the coast with a report on the new arrivals, he sent scouts to all the regions of his empire and then set up what can only be called a war room. Years later, one of the participants remembered: "A report of everything that was happening was given and relayed to Moctezuma. Some of the messengers would be arriving as others were leaving. There was no time when they weren't

The Lienzo de Tlaxcala illustrates the Spaniards' conquest expeditions after the war with the Mexica ended. The people of Tlaxcala were allied with the Europeans.

listening, when reports weren't being given."[1] Some of the messengers even memorized the sermon given by the priest who accompanied Cortés at each village that they visited. Malintzin, a young enslaved woman who spoke Nahuatl, translated it, so the messengers were able to absorb the statements. Later, when the Spaniards arrived in Tenochtitlan and tried to deliver the sermon again, Moctezuma cut them off, explaining that it had already been presented to him in full.[2] Eventually, a great war exploded, and the Mexica and their allies fought tooth and nail against the Spaniards and their allies before they were ultimately defeated.

So where did the story of a fatalistic Moctezuma and his awed people responding to the arrival of a supposed god originate? The only surviving written texts that date from the years 1519–1522 are the letters written by Hernando Cortés, and he at no point claimed that he was perceived as divine. The idea first appeared in the 1540s. In a rather incoherent passage, the Franciscan friar Toribio de Benavente (or "Motolinía") described what Indigenous people were supposed to have thought: "Their god was coming, and because of the white sails, they said he was bringing by sea his own temples." Then the friar remembered that a few pages before he had claimed that all Spaniards were thought to have been gods, so he added, "When [the Spaniards] disembarked, [the Indians] said that it was not their god, but rather many gods."[3] The idea of being worshipped seemed to please the friar, as it did other European colonizers both before and after.

It might seem strange that such an obviously self-serving tale without any contemporary evidence should have grown and then lasted so long, even into the late-twentieth-century years of greater political sensitivity. However, in a fascinating twist, some Indigenous people themselves began to assert the same thing towards the end of the sixteenth century and even more so in the beginning of the seventeenth. The first ones to do so were the students of the very Franciscan friars who had originally developed the tale. They were from noble Indigenous families, and were themselves racked with curiosity and concern about how their once powerful fathers and grandfathers—the same men who had ruled central Mexico—had been brought so low by the newcomers. This story offered a satisfying explanation, an honorable way out of a painful conundrum. It seemed that their progenitors had been capable men after all—just too devout for their own good. The students considered the old stories about the human figure Huemac and about the god Quetzalcoatl (who was indeed associated with the year sign for 1519, among others), mixed them together, emphasizing certain elements and omitting others, and offered narratives that would serve. They accidentally created a problem the first time they presented such a story, insisting that it was the leader of the second expedition that landed on their shores who was interpreted as Quetzalcoatl, but this man was actually Juan de Grijalva, who arrived in 1518. However, the confusion was easily overlooked in future, as the basic elements of the pleasing story were taken up and circulated by Indigenous and European alike.[4]

In fact, there is no early Nahuatl-language story of a human king going away to the east, becoming a god, and being expected to return in 1519 in order to remake the people's lives. The early sixteenth-century Mexica certainly were not waiting to be ruled by the people most devoted to Quetzalcoatl, who in their world were the recently subdued Cholulans (whose temple the Spaniards and Tlaxcalans had ironically burned to the ground on their way to Tenochtitlan). Indeed, the very idea that *anyone* had a pre-ordained right to conquer them would have seemed downright amusing. As the Mexica loved a good joke, perhaps they would have found it funny that so many Europeans were so easily able to convince themselves that this was how they thought about their future, and that they had been so willing to relinquish their kingdom, their gods, and their stories.

TRACES OF THE EARLY YEARS

As the Indigenous got to know the Spaniards and listened to the stories they told, they seem to have experienced not awe, but confusion and alienation. In Cuauhtinchan, one man remembered receiving instructions to go to mass every week. "But no one knew yet what was happening, if it was 'Sunday' [here he threw in the

An ancient carving embedded in the wall of the
Franciscan complex, Calimaya, Mexico.

The Church of San Miguel Arcángel (the Archangel Michael) in the town of Ixmiquilpan, north of Mexico City, was built in the 1560s and 1570s and boasts several multicolored frescoes with obvious Indigenous influence. Here a jaguar warrior battles his enemies.

Spanish word, *domingo*] or some other day. We were really new at it.... We didn't know what was going on."[5] In a history written down by the Tlaxcalans, another man who had been present recalled his early impressions:

There came three of those they called friars. Two of them
gave masses. One was fray Juan [Díaz], one we didn't know
the name of, and the third was called fray Pedro de Gante.
The late Juan was really happy and wanted to teach us,
but he could not yet speak Nahuatl. Up the hill, where
there used to be the market, at the place called Tozcoc,
they placed a big cross. He would stand there, gathering
the people, pointing with his finger at the sky and saying,
"Di-os" and "San-ta María, always a young unmarried
woman." He would point down at the land of the dead,
saying, "Snakes, toads."[6]

This man seems to have been laughing a bit as he told the story, but
others harbored memories that were less benign, recalling that the
Spaniards would hang people whom they even suspected of continuing to practice any part of the old religion. "Then they hanged the
rulers Temiloteuctli, Tlaltochtzin of Quiahuiztlan, Cuauhtotohua
of Atempan, don Francisco Tecpanecatl and Tenamazcuicuiltzin of
Topoyanco. Negligently they killed them. That's the way it was,
there was killing without any reason.… Then began the terror. When
the rulers died, that was when people went for baptism."[7] It seems the
people had not gone to have the priests baptize them out of belief,
but because they were terrified. Not only in Tlaxcala, but in various
places in the mid-sixteenth century, we hear of Indigenous priests of
the old order who wandered the countryside, preaching against the
newcomers and demanding that their people cease to have dealings
with them. One even offered a ceremony that constituted a sort of
reverse baptism, a ceremony that rid the person who underwent it
of any commitments to the new god that he or she might have made.[8]

In the church at Ixmiquilpan, another pre-conquest warrior battles an enemy with a horse's body. Today, substantial numbers of people in the town still speak Nahuatl or Otomí.

Nevertheless, despite the confusion and the strong resistance, the friars persisted. Different religious orders emphasized different elements or made different types of translation choices, but they all moved forward with determination. With the help of Indigenous aides whom they educated, they worked long days—studying Nahuatl, teaching Spanish, and writing sermons, catechisms, commentary, and church plays. Day after day, week after week, year after year, they promoted such projects, and in the end, they met with some success, conveying significant aspects of Christianity to their hearers, especially to the generations born after the arrival of the

Europeans. Translating Christian concepts into terms that worked in Nahuatl was not an easy task and could only be accomplished by a native Spanish speaker and a native Nahuatl speaker working together, reaching for ways to communicate foreign concepts with words and understandings that were available. They had to avoid common words from the old days, like "priest" (tlamacazqui), as such terms were thoroughly bound up with the former ways of thinking and being.

Consider some of the words that they chose to use, or, in some cases, invented:

English	Colonial Spanish	Nahuatl Equivalent	Literal Translation
baptism	bautismo	tecuaatequiliztli	Throwing water on someone's head
believe	creer	neltoca	Follow something true
bishop	obispo	teoyotica tlatoani	Ruler in sacred things
confession	confesión	neyolmelahualiztli	Straightening one's heart
deity	dios	teotl	Deity, something sacred
devil	diablo	tlacatecolotl	A human in the form of a horned owl
heaven	cielo	ilhuicatl	Sky
hell	infierno	mictlan	Land of the dead
salvation	salvación	temaquixtiliztli	Untying of the hands
sin	pecado	tlatlacolli	Something damaged, broken
virgin	virgen	ichpochtli	Young unmarried woman

Table 3 Source: Louise Burkhart, "Christian Doctrine," in *Painted Words*.

There were some terms that simply could not be expressed properly in Nahuatl: grace, Holy Spirit, the name of God, sacrament, saint, soul. For concepts such as these, the Spanish words were used, inserted directly into Nahuatl sentences, and eventually, listeners grew to understand their meaning.[9]

A NEW KIND OF CATHOLICISM?

Within three to four generations, most central Mexicans were at least nominally Catholic. What that meant varied considerably, but due to the untiring efforts of the friars and the secular clergy, more and more Indigenous people gradually came to accept core Christian beliefs. Yet at the same time, they often maintained some of their old religious beliefs alongside the new. On one level, for instance, they learned that this life is preliminary to another, but on another level, they continued to believe that life on earth is special and imbued with the divine, and that they must remember those who had gone before to keep them alive in the way that counted. (To this day, in some Nahuatl-speaking towns, the Day of the Dead rivals Christmas.)

Even some Indigenous disciples of friars who were carefully educated in Christianity could maintain understandings of doctrine that were somewhat distinct from what the friars would have wished. In the mid-sixteenth century, a man who had taken the Christian name of Fabian de Aquino (in honor of Saint Thomas Aquinas) wrote plays about the Antichrist that were somewhat unorthodox. Demons capered across the stage singing in Nahuatl. A large segment of the community would have been involved: One of the plays required fifty-one people to stage it.[10]

Colonial-era Pictorial Catechisms

In the second half of the colonial era, Franciscan friars and their Nahuatl-speaking aides worked together to create Christian pictorial texts loosely inspired by the old glyphic writing system. They hoped these would serve as mnemonic devices that would help non-literate people to engage with Christianity. These images come from a text known as the Atzacualco pictorial catechism. It represents the beginning of the Hail Mary. Following image by image from left to right and top to bottom, we have:

O Saint Mary,	*All*
Rejoice!	*Women.*
You are filled with	*And*
Complete goodness,	*Praiseworthy*
Grace.	*Is your precious child*
With you is	*Jesus Christ.*
The ruler,	*O Saint Mary*
God.	*Maiden*
You are praiseworthy	*Mother of God*
You surpass	

Source of translation: Louise Burkhart, "Deciphering the Catechism," in *Painted Words.*

The opening of the Hail Mary (Ave María)
in the Atzacualco pictorial catechism.

In a later copy of the Annals of Puebla, a talented artist took the
pre-conquest themes of the Nahuatl text and rendered them
creatively using European drawing techniques.

Likewise, the cadence and rhythm of some of the Christian stories
that less educated Indigenous people told often continued to feel
profoundly pre-conquest. In the late seventeenth century, Miguel
de los Santos, a Nahuatl-speaking Indigenous artisan living in the
city of Puebla who helped build churches, wrote the history of his
altepetl, bringing it up to his own day. He described many of the
religious celebrations he witnessed. In 1690, the Dominican order
completed their most splendid chapel. They celebrated by bringing
out on procession a beautiful figure of the Virgin Mary:

> The chapel of our precious revered mother of Rosario
> at [the convent of] Santo Domingo was dedicated. They
> brought her out on Thursday the 14th day of the month
> of April. Then they took her to [the convent of] Santa
> Catarina. There she slept. Then on Friday they took her
> to [the convent of] the Holy Trinity. There she slept. And
> early on Saturday morning they took her to the cathedral,
> and then in the afternoon she came back to her home.

A great many marvels were performed; there were plays
in the streets. On Thursday afternoon, when they brought
her out of her home, a great wind rose. No one went about
any longer, so strong was the wind. As they carried her,
she could no longer be seen.[11]

The writer of these words was a cosmopolitan, urban man deeply
familiar with Christian religious concepts and the story of the holy
Virgin. Yet at the same time, he told her tale much as his ancestors
in that same valley had told the tale of those who left Chicomoztoc
and made their ceremonial passage southward. At each sacred place
they came to, came the rhythmic repetition *cochico*, "there they
slept." These ancestors, too, were beset by wind and weather in their
sacred passage, and they, too, survived and made it home. "Here
ends the road and the days registered for our great grandfathers,
our grandfathers, the children of the Chichimeca," the storyteller
had once intoned.[12]

It was in the next year, 1691, that this same Miguel de los Santos
told the story of a major solar eclipse that opened this chapter. It had
been predicted by a Spanish astronomer, yet despite this, the dramatic
event terrified the city's people. Certain priests rang the church bells
and made the panic worse. As the eclipse passed, don Miguel said he
saw a black figure (*tliltic*) dropping away from the sun and landing
on the mountain called Matlalcueye ("Dark-Green-Skirted One").
He said many people insisted that they saw it, too.[13] Now, the word
tliltic could mean a black object, or a black shape, but by the 1690s,
it almost always meant a black person. Don Miguel seems to have
been implying that he and his compatriots saw a human-like figure
leaving the sun. Could they have had a cultural memory of Ixtlilton

Traditional Pilgrimages

Nahuatl and other Indigenous languages have survived best in Mexico in remote rural areas. The same is true of traditional religious observances. In the Huasteca, a mountainous region north of Veracruz, traditional specialists who bear the title *tlamatiquetl* (person of knowledge) still lead people on pilgrimages to holy sites every year. They cut paper figures for their rituals that embody or reveal the divine, just as holy *amoxtli* (books made from bark paper) did in the sixteenth century. The paper figures, often cut by the thousands, are spattered with the blood of sacrificial chickens or turkeys. At the site, the tlamatiquetl places the figures on flower-decorated altars laden with offerings of food and drink so that the pilgrims can make their petitions (for rainfall, crop fertility, and so on) to the spirit entities revealed in the cut paper.

Beginning in the 1970s, anthropologists Alan and Pamela Sandstrom lived for many months at a time in the Nahuatl-speaking

Ritual specialists Teófilo Jiménez Hernández (second from left) and Cirilo Téllez Hernández (far right) chant before an altar at the start of a pilgrimage to Palaxtepetl ("Male Turkey Mountain") in March 2007.

On the trail to Palaxtepetl. From Sandstrom & Sandstrom, *Pilgrimage to Broken Mountain: Nahua Sacred Journeys in Mexico's Huasteca Veracruzana.*

village of Amatlán in the southern Huasteca. Between 1998 and 2007, they were invited to participate in five different pilgrimages, on the understanding that they would photograph and write about what they observed, in an effort to preserve the practices for the future, in case young people ever let the ceremonies lapse. The leaders of the pilgrimages were the late Encarnación (or Cirilo) Téllez Hernández, a deeply respected ritual specialist, and his apprentice Teófilo Jiménez Hernández. These two were concerned that modern people have been forgetting the bonds that tie them to the natural world. Cirilo said, "These rituals are not a game, they are our life. I am giving you my sons and daughters, my devotion. I spent my life dedicating offerings to them [the divinities], and they provide us with maize. God watches over us when we dig and plant maize, and we have to give something back.... Set up an altar. Follow the correct path."[14] He knew that the religious pilgrimages exemplify the difficulties of following the right path in life—difficulties that have only grown worse in modern times—and he hoped that young people would continue to draw sustenance from knowledge of what their ancestors had done for centuries.

Ixtlilton in the "Primeros Memoriales," an early
draft of the Florentine Codex.

("Little Black One with a Face"), a tiny god who could cure children, who was sometimes called Tlaltetecuini ("Earth Stamper"), and who had shoes that looked like the sun?[15] At the very least, it seems fair to say that in 1690, Miguel de los Santos still lived in a divine universe that showed its magic to mortal eyes in sometimes unexpected ways. The teachings of his ancestors were alive in him.

PROTECTING AND PRESERVING

With so many traditions still vibrant in Mexico's towns and villages, it is not surprising that people in the succeeding centuries repeatedly made efforts to preserve and even revivify Nahuatl language and culture.[16] Their efforts were effective: There are still over a million speakers of Nahuatl in the country, and many others live abroad. Today, the Nahuas of Mexico continue to tell their own stories in their own way. Many of them are now artists and intellectuals, working to write down and analyze all that they can, and to ensure that their people's language and culture will continue far into the future, in an unbroken line rooted in the past. They have much to teach us all.

One of these language activists and writers is Eduardo de la Cruz. He was born in the municipality of Chicontepec ("Seven Hills") in the state of Veracruz and was raised in a community whose maternal tongue was and still is Nahuatl. As a child, De la Cruz lived with both his parents and his grandparents. From them he learned to work the fields and to involve himself in maintaining local customs and beliefs. He completed high school by correspondence. At age eighteen, he left his village in search of opportunities, traveling first to Guadalajara and later to Zacatecas, where he obtained a BA in Economics and a Masters in Humanities Research, both from the Autonomous University of Zacatecas.

During his university years, De la Cruz got to know the Instituto de Docencia e Investigación Etnológica de Zacatecas (IDIEZ), a space where the participants work and speak in their native language. He began to work for IDIEZ in 2010 as an assistant professor of Nahuatl, participating in the project of creating a monolingual (Nahuatl–Nahuatl) dictionary, to serve as the *Oxford English Dictionary* or Webster's does in English. At root, the project rejected the idea that texts in Indigenous languages should immediately be translated into a European tongue. The volume was published in 2016. De la Cruz began to organize courses and workshops right in the midst of the Nahuatl-speaking communities of Chicontepec, as a way of revitalizing and strengthening the language. By 2020, he had become the

Eduardo de la Cruz, like many others of his generation,
is dedicating his professional life to rehabilitating
Nahuatl language, culture, and stories.

director of IDIEZ. His work at the Institute is focused on both teaching and research projects that revitalize Nahuatl language and culture.

Among De la Cruz's many projects is an effort to collaborate with other institutions, such as the Getty Foundation, to bring historic Nahuatl texts (like those in this book) to Nahua school students in a way that will be accessible and appealing to them. Public schools in Mexico do not teach these young people much about their forebears, with the result that they often know very little about the culture of their ancestors, and almost nothing about the strong efforts that they made at the time of conquest to defend that culture. He aims to change all that.

De la Cruz also publishes stories in Nahuatl, as he believes strongly that the oral tradition provides a way of teaching children the knowledge, wisdom and values of a culture. He has preserved those traditions in *Tototatahhuan Ininizxtlamatiliz* (Knowledge of Our Grandparents), published in 2015, and *Cenyahtoc Cintli Tonacayo: huancapatl huan tlen naman* (Corn is Still Our Body: A passage from the past to the present), published in 2017. Sometimes when young Nahuatl-speakers handle one of these books (or likewise a dictionary or a scholarly article written in Nahuatl), it is the first time that they have seen that their mother tongue is also a language of culture and literacy, just like English or Spanish. The experience diminishes the subtle belief with which they have been inculcated, that Indigenous languages are not of great value, and reminds them that there is no thought or philosophy they cannot express in their own tongue.

People living abroad are more than welcome to join the efforts of people living in Mexico to preserve Nahuatl and Nahuatl stories. Language activists like Eduardo de la Cruz welcome all the help they can get. And the world as a whole benefits from keeping alive the endangered traditions of Native Americans, for it is stories in all their wondrous variety that bring us true wisdom.

NOTES

CHAPTER 1

1 Annals of Cuauhtitlan, folio 4.
2 Díaz, *Historia verdadera*, 169.
3 Dibble & Anderson, *Florentine Codex*, 4:20.

4 Olko and Madajczak, "An Animating Principle in Confrontation with Christianity?"
5 See Sorensen, "I am a Singer, I Remember the Lords."

CHAPTER 2

1 Dibble & Anderson, *Florentine Codex*, 7:6.
2 Annals of Cuauhtitlan, folio 2; Legend of the Suns, folio 75.
3 Dibble & Anderson, *Florentine Codex*, 7:4.
4 Andrews, *Classical Nahuatl*, 498.
5 Dibble & Anderson, *Florentine Codex*, 7:4–7.
6 Cantares Mexicanos, folio 22.
7 *Ibid.*, folio 1.
8 Sandstrom, "Flower World," 41. For full discussion, see Maffie, *Aztec Philosophy*.
9 Dibble & Anderson, *Florentine Codex*, 11:29.
10 Chimalpahin in Tena, *Ocho Relaciones*, 1:349.
11 Dibble & Anderson, *Florentine Codex*, 6:160.
12 Lockhart, *The Nahuas after the Conquest*.
13 Dibble & Anderson, *Florentine Codex*, 11:247.
14 Cantares Mexicanos, folio 12.
15 Dibble & Anderson, *Florentine Codex*, 6:35.
16 *Ibid.*, 6:141.
17 Legend of the Suns, folio 76.
18 Annals of Cuauhtitlan, folio 3.

19 Codex Aubin, folio 21v–22. See also Annals of Tlatelolco.
20 Annals of Cuauhtitlan, folios 1 and 4.
21 Dibble & Anderson, *Florentine Codex*, 4:11.
22 Legend of the Suns, folios 78–80.
23 *Ibid.*; Florentine Codex 3; and Annals of Cuauhtitlan, folios 3–5.
24 Annals of Cuauhtitlan, folio 7.
25 Dibble & Anderson, *Florentine Codex*, 3:1–5
26 Montero Sobrevilla, "The Disguise of the Hummingbird."
27 Codex Chimalpahin, 1:77–83.
28 *Ibid.*, 1:83–87; and Tena, *Ocho Relaciones*, 1:159.
29 Dibble & Anderson, *Florentine Codex*, 6:94.
30 Cantares Mexicanos, folio 13.
31 Dibble & Anderson, *Florentine Codex*, 2:53.
32 *Ibid.*, 2:184–85.
33 *Ibid.*, 6:242.
34 *Ibid.*, 6:162–63.
35 *Ibid.*, 3:45 and 4:115.
36 Cantares Mexicanos, folio 12.
37 Dibble & Anderson, *Florentine Codex*, 3:42.

CHAPTER 3

1 Annals of Tlatelolco, folio 8.
2 Codex Chimalpahin, 1:120–21.
3 Legends of the Suns, folios 82–83; Chimalpahin in Tena, *Ocho Relaciones*, 1:77; Dibble & Anderson, *Florentine Codex*, 3:17–21; and Annals of Cuauhtitlan, folios 8–11.
4 Historia Tolteca Chichimeca, folio 11.
5 *Ibid.*, folio 12.
6 For more, see Andrews, *Classical Nahuatl*, 496.
7 Codex Aubin, folios 3–8; Annals of Tlatelolco, folios 6–7; Codex Chimalpahin, 1:71; and Chimalpahin in Tena, *Ocho Relaciones*, 183–85.
8 Codex Aubin, folio 19v.
9 Annals of Tlatelolco, folio 8. See also Codex Aubin, folio 19v; and Chimalpahin in Tena, *Ocho Relaciones*, 1:167 and 351.
10 Codex Chimalpahin, 1:93.
11 Annals of Tlatelolco, folios 8–9. See also Codex Aubin, folio 20; and Chimalpahin in Tena, *Ocho Relaciones*, 1:169.

12 Annals of Tlatelolco, folio 9. See also Codex Aubin, folio 22.
13 Codex Aubin, folio 22.
14 Annals of Tlatelolco, folio 9.
15 Chimalpahin in Tena, *Ocho Relaciones*, 213. See also Codex Aubin and Codex Chimalpahin, 1:101.
16 Historia Tolteca Chichimeca, folios 17–19.
17 Annals of don Juan Buenaventura Zapata y Mendoza, folio 1. See also Chimalpahin in Tena, *Ocho Relaciones*, 1:211.
18 Annals of Cuauhtitlan, folio 1.
19 *Ibid.*, folio 10.
20 *Ibid.*, folio 13.
21 *Ibid.*, folio 14.
22 *Ibid.*, folio 17.
23 *Ibid.*, folios 21–22.
24 *Ibid.*, folio 23.
25 Díaz, *Historia verdadera*, 159.
26 Codex Chimalpahin, 1:61.
27 Codex Aubin, folio 26; See also Zapata y Mendoza, Annals of Tlaxcala, folio 2v.
28 Dibble & Anderson, *Florentine Codex*, 6:8–9.

CHAPTER 4

1 Codex Chimalpahin, 1:118–25.
2 Annals of Cuauhtitlan, folio 17.
3 Chimalpahin in Tena, *Ocho Relaciones*, 1:343.
4 For instance: Historia Tolteca Chichimeca, folio 47v.
5 Annals of Cuauhtitlan, folio 17.
6 Dibble & Anderson, *Florentine Codex*, 6:127–33.
7 Annals of Cuauhtitlan, folio 33.
8 See the Texcocan narratives in Codex Chimalpahin, 2.
9 Annals of Cuauhtitlan, folio 34.

10 Historia Tolteca Chichimeca, folio 43v.
11 See Florentine Codex 6 and Bancroft Dialogues.
12 Dibble & Anderson, *Florentine Codex*, 6:248.
13 Codex Chimalpahin, 1:207–209.
14 For instance: Reyes, *Anales de Juan Bautista*, 236–37.
15 Dibble & Anderson, *Florentine Codex*, 6:41, 47, and 53.
16 *Ibid.*, 6:35.
17 *Ibid.*, 6:4–5.

18 Codex Chimalpahin, 1:115–17. See also Annals of Tlatelolco and Annals of Cuauhtitlan.
19 Codex Chimalpahin, 1:119–23. See Schroeder, "The First American Valentine."
20 Chimalpahin in Tena, *Ocho Relaciones*, 1:365–75.
21 *Ibid.*, 1:383–85.
22 Codex Chimalpahin, 2:53–55.
23 Annals of Cuauhtitlan, folios 43–44. See also Annals of Tlatelolco.
24 Codex Aubin, folio 35.
25 Annals of Tlatelolco, folio 13v.
26 Codex Chimalpahin, 1:137.
27 For ex: Historia Tolteca Chichimeca, folio 44v.
28 Chimalpahin in Tena, *Ocho Relaciones*, 2:84–97.
29 Therrell, Stahle & Acuña Soto, "Aztec Drought and the 'Curse of One Rabbit.'"
30 Annals of Tlatelolco, folio 14.
31 Chimalpahin in Tena, *Ocho Relaciones*, 2:101; Codex Chimalpahin, 2:46–47.
32 Annals of Cuauhtitlan, folio 56.
33 Codex Chimalpahin, 1:136–39.
34 *Ibid.*, 2:44–45.
35 *Ibid.*, 2:50–51.
36 Zapata y Mendoza, folio 3.
37 *Ibid.*, folio 3v.
38 Annals of Cuauhtitlan, folio 58. See also Chimalpahin, Zapata y Mendoza and others.

CHAPTER 5

1 Chimalpahin in Tena, *Ocho Relaciones*, 2:137–39. See also Codex Chimalpahin, 1:53.
2 Cantares Mexicanos, folio 13.
3 Jorge Klor de Alva, Preface to León-Portilla, *The Broken Spears*.
4 León-Portilla, *Aztec Thought and Culture*, xxi.
5 Dibble & Anderson, *Florentine Codex*, 6:155.
6 *Ibid.*, 10:30.
7 *Ibid.*, 6:160. See Chapter 2.
8 Dibble & Anderson, *Florentine Codex*, 6:167–68. (Translation amended.)
9 *Ibid.*, 4:61.
10 *Ibid.*, 3:63–64.
11 *Ibid.*, 7:17–18.
12 Chimalpahin in Tena, *Ocho Relaciones*, 1:355 and 2:137.
13 Annals of Cuauhtitlan, folio 23.
14 *Ibid.*, folios 61–62.
15 Dibble & Anderson, *Florentine Codex*, 6:197–98.
16 *Ibid.*, 4:95–96
17 Townsend, *Here in This Year*, 73 (*yn icuac motlatlalo mixcoatl ytech ylhuicatl*).
18 See Chapter 2.
19 Dibble & Anderson, *Florentine Codex*, 4:41, 81, 155, 171, 192, and 195.
20 *Ibid.*, 2:53.
21 Durán, *Historia de las Indias*, 1:174. The timing is logical; it could not have been before.
22 Dibble & Anderson, *Florentine Codex*, 2:129.
23 See the Lenape story "Ball Player," in Townsend and Michael, *On the Turtle's Back*.
24 Chimalpahin in Tena, *Ocho Relaciones*.
25 Chimalpahin comments on this as well. See Schroeder et al., *Chimalpahin's Conquest*, 192.
26 Dibble & Anderson, *Florentine Codex*, 2:111.
27 Leonardo López Luján, Raúl Barrera Rodríguez, and Ximena Chávez Balderas, speaking at "Tenochtitlan: Imperial Ideologies on Display,"

Dumbarton Oaks, Washington, D.C.,
8 April 2022.

28 Chimalpahin in Tena, *Ocho Relaciones*,
2:143.

29 Annals of Cuauhtitlan, folio 9.

30 Dibble & Anderson, *Florentine Codex*,
2:145, 153, 156, 188–89, and 192.

31 *Ibid.*, 2:185.

32 *Ibid.*, 3:6.

CHAPTER 6

1 Florentine Codex 12 in Lockhart, *We People Here*, 94.

2 Díaz, *Historia verdadera*, 165.

3 Motolinía, *Historia de los Indios*, 102–108.

4 Townsend, "Burying the White Gods."

5 Medina Lima, *Libro de Guardianes*, 36.

6 Zapata y Mendoza, folio 3v.

7 *Ibid.*, folio 4v.

8 Annals of Juan Bautista, folio 8. For more, see Mendoza, "Painting Colonialism with Words."

9 For a key study, see Burkhart, *Slippery Earth.*

10 Leeming, *Aztec Antichrist.*

11 Townsend, *Here in This Year*, 149.

12 Historia Tolteca Chichimeca, folios 23–26.

13 Townsend, *Here in This Year*, 155.

14 Sandstrom & Sandstrom, *Pilgrimage*, 3.

15 Dibble & Anderson, *Florentine Codex*, 1:15–16.

16 See McDonough, *The Learned Ones.*

BIBLIOGRAPHY

PRIMARY NAHUATL SOURCES

Codex Aubin (British Museum, London).

Bancroft Dialogues (Bancroft Library, University of California, Berkeley).

Cantares Mexicanos (Biblioteca Nacional, Mexico City).

Codex Chimalpahin (Instituto Nacional de Antropología e Historia [INAH], Mexico City).

Chimalpahin's "Eight Relations" (Bibliothèque nationale de France [BnF], Paris).

Annals of Cuauhtitlan (original now lost, Velázquez facsimile).

Florentine Codex (Biblioteca Medicea Laurenziana, Florence).

Annals of Juan Bautista (Biblioteca Lorenzo Boturini, Mexico City).

Legend of the Suns (original now lost, Velázquez facsimile).

Libro de Guardianes (Universidad Nacional Autónoma de México, Mexico City).

Annals of Puebla (INAH, Mexico City).

Annals of Tecamachalco (Nettie Lee Benson Collection, University of Texas, Austin).

Hernando Alvarado Tezozomoc (within Codex Chimalpahin).

Annals of Tlatelolco (BnF, Paris).

Annals of Tlaxcala (INAH, Mexico City).

Historia Tolteca Chichimeca (BnF, Paris).

Juan Buenaventura Zapata y Mendoza (BnF, Paris).

PUBLISHED PRIMARY SOURCES TRANSLATED FROM NAHUATL

Anderson, Arthur J.O.; and Susan Schroeder, eds. *Codex Chimalpahin*, vols 1–2. Norman: University of Oklahoma Press, 1997.

Bierhorst, John, ed. *Cantares Mexicanos*. Stanford: Stanford University Press, 1985.

Bierhorst, John, ed. *History and Mythology of the Aztecs: The Codex Chimalpopoca* [Annals of Cuauhtitlan and the Legend of the Suns]. Tucson: University of Arizona Press, 1992.

Dibble, Charles; and Arthur J.O. Anderson, eds. *Florentine Codex: General History of the Things of New Spain*, vols 1–12. Santa Fe, New Mexico: School of American Research, 1950–82.

Dibble, Charles, ed. *Historia de la Nación Mexicana* [Codex Aubin]. Madrid: Porrúa, 1963.

Karttunen, Frances; and James Lockhart, eds. *The Art of Nahuatl Speech: The Bancroft Dialogues*. Los Angeles: UCLA Latin American Center, 1987.

Kirchoff, Paul; Lina Odena Güemes; and Luis Reyes García, eds. *Historia Tolteca Chichimeca*. Mexico City: INAH, 1976.

Medina Lima, Constantino, ed. *Libro de Guardianes y gobernadores de Cuauhtinchan*. Mexico City: CIESAS, 1995.

Reyes García, Luis, ed. *¿Cómo te confundes? ¿Acaso no somos conquistados? Anales de Juan Bautista*. Mexico City: CIESAS, 2001.

Reyes García, Luis; and Andrea Martínez Baracs, eds. *Juan Buenaventura Zapata y Mendoza: Historia cronológica de la Noble Ciudad de Tlaxcala*. Tlaxcala: Universidad Autónoma de Tlaxcala, 1995.

Schroeder, Susan; Anne J. Cruz; Cristián Roa-de-la-Carrera; and David Tavárez, eds. *Chimalpahin's Conquest: A Nahua Historian's Rewriting of Francisco López de Gómara's "La Conqista de México"*. Stanford: Stanford University Press, 2010.

Tena, Rafael, ed. *Anales de Tlatelolco*. Mexico City: CONACULTA, 2004.

Tena, Rafael, ed. *Ocho Relaciones y el memorial de Culhuacan*, vols 1–2. Mexico City: CONACULTA, 1998.

Townsend, Camilla, ed. *Here in This Year: Seventeenth-Century Nahuatl Annals of the Tlaxcala-Puebla Valley*. Stanford: Stanford University Press, 2010.

Velázquez, Primo Feliciano. *Códice Chimalpopoca: Anales de Cuauhtitlan y Leyenda de los soles*. Mexico City: Imprenta Universitaria, 1945.

PRIMARY SPANISH SOURCES

Díaz, Bernal. *Historia verdadera de la conquista de la Nueva España*. Mexico City: Porrúa, 2000.

Durán, fray Diego. *Historia de las Indias*, vols 1–2. Mexico City: Ignacio Escalante, 1867 and 1880.

Motolinía, fray Toribio de Benavente. *Historia de los indios de la Nueva España*. Madrid: Alianza, 1988.

FURTHER READING IN ENGLISH

Andrews, Richard. *An Introduction to Classical Nahuatl.* Norman: University of Oklahoma Press, 2004.

Berdan, Frances. *Aztec Archaeology and Ethnohistory.* New York and London: Cambridge University Press, 2014.

Boone, Elizabeth Hill. *Stories in Red and Black: Pictorial Histories of the Aztecs and Mixtecs.* Austin: University of Texas Press, 2000.

Burkhart, Louise. *Slippery Earth: Nahua-Christian Moral Dialogue in Sixteenth-Century Mexico.* Tucson: University of Arizona Press, 1989.

Burkhart, Louise. "Christian Doctrine: Nahuas Encounter the Catechism" and "Deciphering the Catechism," in *Painted Words: Nahua Catholicism, Politics, and Memory in the Atzaqualco Pictorial Catechism,* ed. by Elizabeth Hill Boone, Louise Burkhart and David Tavárez. Washington, D.C.: Dumbarton Oaks, 2017.

Carmack, Robert; Janine Gasco; and Gary Gossen. *The Legacy of Mesoamerica: History and Culture of a Native American Civilization.* Upper Saddle River, NJ: Prentice Hall, 2007.

Carrasco, Davíd; and Scott Sessions. *Daily Life of the Aztecs.* Indianapolis: Hackett Publishing, 2008.

Edmonson, Munro. *The Book of the Year: Middle American Calendrical Systems.* Salt Lake City: University of Utah Press, 1988.

Evans, Susan Toby. *Ancient Mexico and Central America.* London and New York: Thames & Hudson, 2013.

Haskett, Robert. *Visions of Paradise: Primordial Titles and Mesoamerican*

History in Cuernavaca. Norman: University of Oklahoma Press, 2005.

Jeffres, Travis. *The Forgotten Diaspora: Mesoamerican Migrations and the Making of the US–Mexico Borderlands.* Lincoln: University of Nebraska Press, 2023.

Karttunen, Frances. *An Analytical Dictionary of Nahuatl.* Norman: University of Oklahoma, 1992.

Leeming, Ben. *Aztec Antichrist: Performing the Apocalypse in Early Colonial Mexico.* Boulder: University Press of Colorado, 2022.

Leibsohn, Dana. *Script and Glyph: Pre-Hispanic History, Colonial Bookmaking and the Historia Tolteca-Chichimeca.* Washington, D.C.: Dumbarton Oaks, 2009.

León-Portilla, Miguel. *Aztec Thought and Culture.* Norman: University of Oklahoma Press, 1963 [1956].

León-Portilla, Miguel. *The Broken Spears: The Aztec Account of the Conquest of Mexico.* Boston: Beacon Press, 1970.

Lockhart, James. *The Nahuas after the Conquest.* Stanford: Stanford University Press, 1992.

Lockhart, James. *We People Here: Nahuatl Accounts of the Conquest of Mexico.* Berkeley: University of California Press, 1993.

López Austín, Alfredo. *Tamoanchan, Tlalocan: Places of Mist.* Boulder: University Press of Colorado, 1997.

Maffie, James. *Aztec Philosophy: Understanding a World in Motion.* Boulder: University Press of Colorado, 2014.

Malanga, Tara. "'Earth is No One's Home': Nahua Perceptions of Illness, Death and Dying in the Early Colonial Period." PhD dissertation, Department of History, Rutgers University, 2020.

Mathiowetz, Michael; and Andrew Turner, eds. *Flower Worlds: Religion, Aesthetics, and Ideology in Mesoamerica and the American Southwest.* Tucson: University of Arizona Press, 2021.

Matos Moctezuma, Eduardo. *Life and Death in the Templo Mayor.* Boulder: University Press of Colorado, 1995.

McDonough, Kelly. *The Learned Ones: Nahua Intellectuals in Post-Conquest Mexico.* Tucson: University of Arizona Press, 2014.

Mendoza, Celso. "Painting Colonialism with Words: The Aztecs Recording and Resisting Spanish Rule a Generation after Conquest." PhD dissertation, Department of History, Rutgers University, 2023.

Miller, Mary; and Karl Taube. *An Illustrated Dictionary of the Gods and Symbols of Ancient Mexico and the Maya.* London and New York: Thames & Hudson, 1997.

Montero Sobrevilla, Iris. "The Disguise of the Hummingbird: On the Natural History of Huitzilopochtli in the Florentine Codex." *Ethnohistory* 67 (July 2020).

Mundy, Barbara. *The Death of Aztec Tenochtitlan, the Life of Mexico City.* Austin: University of Texas Press, 2015.

Navarrete Linares, Federico. "Tlaxcalan Histories of the Conquest and the Construction of Cultural Memory." *Iberoamericana* 19 (2019): 35–50.

Olivier, Guilhem. *Mockeries and Metamorphoses of an Aztec God: Tezcatlipoca, Lord of the Smoking Mirror.* Boulder: University Press of Colorado, 2003.

Olivier, Guilhem. "Humans and Gods in the Mexica Universe," in *The Oxford Handbook of the Aztecs.* New York and London: Oxford University Press, 2017.

Olko, Justyna; and Julia Madajczak. "An Animating Principle in Confrontation with Christianity? De(Re)Constructing the Nahua 'Soul.'" *Ancient Mesoamerica* 30 (2019).

Oudijk, Michael; and María Castañeda de Paz. "Nahua Thought and the Conquest," in *The Oxford Handbook of the Aztecs.* New York and London: Oxford University Press, 2017.

Pizzigoni, Caterina. "Where Did All the Angels Go? An Interpretation of the Nahua Supernatural World," in *Angels, Demons and the New World*, ed. by Fernando Cervantes and Andrew Radden. Cambridge: Cambridge University Press, 2013.

Rajagopalan, Angela Herren. *Portraying the Aztec Past: The Codices Boturini, Azcatlitlan, and Aubin.* Austin: University of Texas Press, 2019.

Read, Kay Almere; and Jason González. *Mesoamerican Mythology.* New York: Oxford University Press, 2000.

Ruiz Medrano, Ethelia. *Mexico's Indigenous Communities: Their Lands and Histories, 1500–2010.* Boulder: University Press of Colorado, 2010.

Sandstrom, Alan. "Flower World in the Religious Ideology of Contemporary Nahua of the Southern Huasteca," in *Flower Worlds: Religion, Aesthetics, and Ideology in Mesoamerica and the American Southwest*, ed. by Michael Mathiowetz and Andrew Turner. Tucson: University of Arizona Press, 2021.

Sandstrom, Alan; and Pamela Effrein Sandstrom. *Pilgrimage to Broken Mountain: Nahua Sacred Journeys in Mexico's Huasteca Veracruzana.* Denver: University Press of Colorado, 2022.

Schroeder, Susan. "The First American Valentine: Nahua Courtship and Other

Aspects of Family Structuring in Mesoamerica." *Journal of Family History* 23 (1998).

Smith, Michael. *The Aztecs*. Oxford: Blackwell Publishers, 1996.

Sorensen, Peter Bjorndahl. "'I am a Singer, I Remember the Lords': History in the Sixteenth-Century Aztec Cantares." PhD dissertation, Department of History, Rutgers University, 2022.

Tavárez, David. *The Invisible War: Indigenous Devotions, Discipline, and Dissent in Colonial Mexico*. Stanford: Stanford University Press, 2011.

Therrell, Matthew; David W. Stahle; and Rodolfo Acuña Soto. "Aztec Drought and the 'Curse of One Rabbit.'"*Bulletin of the American Meteorological Society* 85(9) (September 2004).

Townsend, Camilla. "Burying the White Gods: New Perspectives on the Conquest of Mexico." *American Historical Review* 108 (2003).

Townsend, Camilla. *Annals of Native America: How the Nahuas of Colonial Mexico Kept Their History Alive*. New York: Oxford University Press, 2017.

Townsend, Camilla. *Fifth Sun: A New History of the Aztecs*. New York: Oxford University Press, 2020.

Townsend, Camilla; and Nicky Kay Michael. *On the Turtle's Back: Stories the Lenape Told Their Grandchildren*. New Brunswick, NJ: Rutgers University Press, 2023.

Whittaker, Gordon. *Deciphering Aztec Hieroglyphs: A Guide to Nahuatl Writing*. London: Thames & Hudson, 2021.

Wood, Stephanie. *Transcending Conquest: Nahua Views of Spanish Colonial Mexico*. Norman: University of Oklahoma Press, 2003.

ACKNOWLEDGMENTS

This book has been a joy to write. At Thames & Hudson, I thank Ben Hayes, who always seemed to share my vision, as well as Jen Moore and Louise Thomas, editors extraordinaire of word and image, respectively. Over the course of about a year, I benefited immensely from questions posed by audience members when I gave talks at McGill, Northwestern, Northern Illinois University, Ann Arbor, and the Embassy of Mexico. Thank you for pushing me! Two generous souls offered to serve as early readers: I am profoundly grateful to John Nolan and Josh Anthony for their critiques. Meanwhile, I have gained more than I can say in recent months from the scholarship and friendship of colleagues who have discussed Nahua religion and other matters with me, especially Louise Burkhart, Lidia Gómez, Jim Maffie, Caterina Pizzigoni, Ethelia Ruiz-Medrano, and Alan and Pamela Sandstrom. Above all, I am indebted to the ongoing work of two fluent Nahuatlatos: Rafael Tena and Eduardo de la Cruz.

Those wishing to volunteer to help Eduardo de la Cruz in his work at IDIEZ can reach him at xochiayotzin@gmail.com.

SOURCES OF ILLUSTRATIONS

a = above; b = below; l = left; r = right

1 Dumbarton Oaks, Research Library and Collection, Washington, D.C./DeAgostini/ Getty Images; **2** Peter M. Wilson/Alamy Stock Photo; **10** Photo Magnus von Koeller; **11** Art Institute of Chicago: Through prior gifts of Mr. and Mrs. Arthur M. Wood and Mr. and Mrs. William E. Hartmann; Robert Allerton Trust; through prior gifts of Ethel and Julian R. Goldsmith and Mr. and Mrs. Samuel A. Marx; Morris L. Parker Fund; purchased with funds provided by Cynthia and Terry Perucca and Bill and Stephanie Sick; Wirt D. Walker Trust, Bessie Bennett, and Elizabeth R. Vaughn funds; purchased with funds provided by Rita and Jim Knox and Susan and Stuart Handler; Edward E. Ayer Fund in memory of Charles L. Hutchinson and Gladys N. Anderson Fund; purchased with funds provided by Terry McGuire; Samuel P. Avery and Charles U. Harris Endowed Acquisition funds (2012.2); **12–13** Max Shen/Moment/Getty Images; **14a** Suzuki Kaku/Alamy Stock Photo; **14b** Los Angeles County Museum of Art: Gift of Constance McCormick Fearing (AC1996.146.56); **16** Art Institute of Chicago: Gift of Joseph P. Antonow (1962.1073); **17** G. Dagli Orti/De Agostini Picture Library/akg-images; **18** Sahagún, Bernardino De, *General History of the Things of New Spain by Fray Bernardino de Sahagún: The Florentine Codex. Book XI: Natural Things*, 1577. Retrieved from the Library of Congress, Washington, D.C. (2021667856); **22** Art Nick/Shutterstock; **23** Album/Alamy Stock Photo; **26** Fordham University, New York; **28** Werner Forman/Universal Images Group/Getty Images; **31** © The Trustees of the British Museum, London; **35** Photo El Comandante; **37** Illustration courtesy Professor Dr. Gordon Whittaker, from *Deciphering Aztec Hieroglyphs* (Thames & Hudson, 2021); **39** Sahagún, Bernardino De, *General History of the Things of New Spain by Fray Bernardino de Sahagún: The Florentine Codex. Book VII: The Sun, Moon, and Stars, and the Binding of the Years*, 1577. Retrieved from the Library of Congress, Washington, D.C. (2021667852); **41** Foundation for the Advancement of Mesoamerican Studies, Inc.; **42** Sahagún, Bernardino De, *General History of the Things of New Spain by Fray Bernardino de Sahagún: The Florentine Codex. Book XI: Natural Things*, 1577. Retrieved from the Library of Congress, Washington, D.C. (2021667856); **47a** Fordham University, New York; **47b** *Paintings of the Governor, Mayors and Rulers of Mexico*, 1565. Retrieved from the Library of Congress, Washington, D.C. (202166702); **48, 50** Foundation for the Advancement of Mesoamerican Studies, Inc.; **51l** Musée de l'Homme, Paris/Bridgeman Images; **51r** © The Trustees of the British Museum, London; **52** The Picture Art Collection/Alamy Stock Photo; **55** Fordham University, New York; **56** Bibliothèque nationale de France, Paris (Mexicain 46–58); **60** Museum für Völkerkunde, Vienna/Bridgeman Images; **61** Wang LiQiang/Shutterstock; **62** Sahagún, Bernardino De, *General History of the Things of New Spain by Fray Bernardino de Sahagún: The Florentine Codex. Book XI: Natural Things*, 1577. Retrieved from the Library of Congress, Washington, D.C. (2021667856); **65** Photo Dennis Jarvis, Halifax, Nova Scotia; **68** Photo Gary Todd, Xinzheng; **69** Foundation for the Advancement of Mesoamerican Studies, Inc.;

INDEX

Page numbers in *italics* refer to illustrations.